IT TAKES TWO

IT TAKES TWO
The Joy of Intimate Marriage

Andrew D. Lester
Judith L. Lester

Westminster John Knox Press
Louisville, Kentucky

Scripture quotations from the New Revised Standard Version of the Bible are copyright © 1989 by the Division of Christian Education of the National Council of the Churches of Christ in the U.S.A. and are used by permission.

Book and cover design by Jennifer K. Cox
Cover photo by Bill Miles. Courtesy of The Stock Market

First Edition
Published by Westminster John Knox Press
Louisville, Kentucky

This book is printed on acid-free paper that meets the American National Standards Institute Z39.48 standard. ♾

PRINTED IN THE UNITED STATES OF AMERICA
98 99 00 01 02 03 04 05 06 07—10 9 8 7 6 5 4 3 2 1

Library of Congress Cataloging-in-Publication Data

Lester, Andrew D.
    It takes two : the joy of intimate marriage / Andrew D. Lester,
Judith L. Lester. — 1st ed.
        p.   cm.
    Includes bibliographical references.
    ISBN 0-664-25594-9 (alk. paper)
    1. Married people—Religious life.   2. Marriage—Religious aspects—Christianity.
3. Intimacy (Psychology)—Religious aspects—Christianity.   4. Lester, Andrew D.
5. Lester, Judith L., 1940.   I. Lester, Judith L., 1940.   II. Title.
BV4596.M3L47   1998
248.8'44—dc21   97-50587

To our children and their partners

Scott and Mary Beth
Denise and David

Both our children, Scott and Denise, became engaged while we were finishing this book. We delight in the love they share and are excited to welcome Mary Beth and David into our family. This book is dedicated to these two couples and their future stories.

Contents

Acknowledgments

We want to express our appreciation to those who have shared themselves with us in the context of counseling relationships. We admire your willingness to struggle with yourselves and your partners in order to create more intimate marriages. It has been our privilege to participate in many transformations and reconciliations. Those of you who divorced also taught us significant ideas about intimacy in marriage.

We also thank the couples in our marriage enrichment classes and participants in marriage enrichment events sponsored by churches and religious institutions for trusting us with so many stories (many of which are scattered through this book) and for allowing us to participate in the process by which you were enriching your relationship.

We express our appreciation for friends and colleagues who were willing to read all or parts of various drafts of this manuscript: Shirley Bubar, Amy Cooper, Dawn Darwin, Larry Easterling, Robin Gray, Irene Henderson, Ginny Henley, Cannan Hyde, James Hyde, Denise Lester, Ann Sanders, Charles Sanders, and Frank Thomas. They offered critique which enabled us to sharpen our concepts and clarify our expressions. Stephanie Egnotovich, Managing Editor of Westminster John Knox Press, convinced us that this project was worthwhile, then offered encouragement throughout the process and understood our delays. Nick Street consulted about the final editing, listening carefully and offering thoughtful suggestions that have strengthened the final presentation.

Happily Ever After?
An Introduction

We plead guilty. We gave magical powers to marriage. We assumed that repeating the vows and exchanging the rings at our wedding would automatically, as in fairy tales, allow us to "live happily ever after." We were thoroughly indoctrinated with the myth of romantic love. We had seen the movies that end with the loving couple magically floating toward a destiny of unimaginable bliss. For us, this picture of marriage lasted for several months (or was it weeks?) before reality showed up. It came in the form of conflict that we were incompetent to handle creatively, leaving us disillusioned and distant. We were frightened when our love boat on the never-ending sea of romance ran aground, worried that something was wrong with us if we could not attain the perfect, ever-romantic marriage. Furthermore, we had made our vows before God, as well as family and friends, and were concerned about what our failures communicated about our Christian faith and commitments.

After several years of feeling guilty that our marriage was not perfect, we enrolled in a graduate course on marriage and family. We learned many helpful concepts, but the most important was the idea that marriages are dynamic, not static. Marriages are like people: they must grow and develop. We don't begin married life as a mature couple. We don't step into a fully developed relationship. Somehow the two of us had adopted the belief that courtship was the hard part and that when we got married everything would come up roses.

When the well-known verse from Genesis suggests that men and women "become one flesh," it sounds so easy. In fact, as all couples learn, becoming "one flesh"—which we interpret to mean establishing a mutually meaningful, loving, intimate relationship—is no easy task!

We learned that a marriage is a living entity. It has a life of its own that must be nourished and nurtured. We can be as intentional about growing our marital relationship as we are about growing spiritually. Maturing a marriage is a lifelong process, a journey. Every day provides opportunities for us to grow and develop, coming closer to the full potential for intimacy that God has made possible in marriage. This was a wonderful revelation for us—God is not expecting perfection but intentional nurturing on a daily basis.

Most of us learn two contradictory messages about marriage. On the one hand, we learn the myth of romantic love, that somewhere out there is the perfect mate with whom we will fall in love and live happily ever after. On the other hand, we learn from watching those married persons around us, usually including our own parents, that marriage isn't perfect. Despite evidence to the contrary, most of us enter marriage believing that we will beat the odds and attain that elusive ideal marriage, the perfect relationship that offers intimate companionship, ecstatic sexual fulfillment, and never-ending romance. Every partnership, however, runs aground on the realities of normal life in which our human frailties make it impossible to meet these exaggerated expectations. The result is some level of frustration and disillusionment.

Now what? You depended on the "love" you felt toward your partner to be the magic that made the perfect marriage. Now that the marriage isn't perfect, does that mean that you are no longer in love? Not necessarily, but it does mean that you have to give attention to the "work" of being happily married. Whatever the actual words, when you exchanged vows at the wedding you pledged your steadfast and faithful love to each other. Now you must determine how to fulfill that vow.

WHY READ THIS BOOK?

The institution of marriage does not come with an instruction booklet, nor with guarantees for a lifetime of bliss. The marriage license is given in return for money, not for documentation of competence. The state requires no proof of education, readiness, maturation, or ability. You don't have to submit a certificate of training, provide a transcript of courses taken, study any manuals, or take any tests. Churches rarely require more than a visit with the clergyperson, though some, to their credit, offer effective "preparation for marriage" programs. Our culture seems to assume that being happily married comes naturally. Wrong!

Love has to be directed. It has to be informed and educated. Marriage requires intentional focus of thought and behavior. You can enjoy an intimate marriage if you take responsibility for creating one, rather than leaving that up to luck or fate. We have both the opportunity and the responsibility for making marriage into a fulfilling, meaningful, intimate relationship. Within our marriages we have more freedom than in most arenas of life to create something that is uniquely ours, with commitments and expectations established by our own design.

This book is written as a guide to couples who are taking responsibility for deepening their relationship. We offer the contents to use as a guide while you are seeking to expand your understanding and pursuit of intimacy.

WHO ARE YOU?

Who are you, the reader? We have written material that we hope will help four groups:

- Some of you are engaged or newly married and eagerly pursuing information about nurturing a Christian marriage. Others are considering a commitment to marry for the second or third time (due to death or divorce) and want help in making this next marriage different. You are seeking ideas about creating an intimate marriage from its outset.

  For you this book will be educational, an eye-opening encounter with those dynamics of marriage that can be followed as paths into intimacy. The exercises will introduce you to levels of intimacy that you have not yet experienced and serve as a preventive shield against alienation and unnecessary conflict.

- Many of you are in good, stable, happy marriages that you care about protecting and enriching. You are involved in seeking deeper levels of understanding and intimacy. Looking for new ways to express your love is part of your ongoing commitment to the relationship.

We trust that the ideas expressed in this book will guide your search. The exercises will direct you toward new horizons of intimacy.

- Others of you are reading this after being married a few years, and the bloom has fallen off the flower. Though you would consider your marriage a good one and are glad to be married to this partner, you are trying to deal with an unmistakable sense of boredom, disappointment, and dissatisfaction that is making you feel uncomfortable and vulnerable at the same time. You feel frustrated because the ideal expectations, the anticipated future you hoped for, have not come to pass. One friend describes this as the "kind of happy but you know it could be better" state of marriage. You are looking for ideas for restoring the excitement and passion that once energized the relationship.

  When rooted in the original excitement and commitment, marriages can mature over the years and become a source of nurture, enjoyment, and support for both partners. Perhaps you trust your partner and the relationship enough to make your doubts and concerns an open agenda and invite her or him to make this pilgrimage toward enrichment. This book will provide ideas that might help you understand what attitudes and behaviors have been eating away at the happiness you once enjoyed. It will offer guidance on how to address those aspects of marriage that have not received the attention needed to produce an intimate relationship.

- Some of you may have discovered that your marriage only survives because of inertia, or for the sake of the children, or because of a pattern of enmeshment that you had not realized. You have decided that you want something better. Other readers may be in more desperate circumstances, reading this book because your marriage is passing through a crisis that seriously threatens the future of the relationship such as an affair, unemployment, going back to school, unexpected pregnancy, or the death of a child or parent. This stress has accentuated the most disturbing elements in each partner's personality and caused significant friction. The anger is expressed in blaming and accusation, leading to resentment and bitterness. A chronic level of hostility may pervade the marriage, making being together uncomfortable for you, the children, and even friends. Perhaps the chasm that separates you from one another has led you into despair and hopelessness, a chronic sadness about the loss of something that was once important.

Our hope is that this book will provide insight into what went wrong, and offer some new understandings about the dynamics that are preventing intimacy and destroying the relationship. Perhaps these ideas will empower you to confront the issues and change your behavior in such a manner that your new way of relating invites your partner to work with you. Through God's grace there is the potential for reconciliation. Transformation *is* possible.

WHERE ARE WE COMING FROM?

Who are we, the authors? What shapes our ideas about marriage? How did we decide what issues to tackle, what themes are important, and what processes are most creative and redemptive for couples? We bring into this book perceptions and clinical illustrations from several sources.

- Being married to one another for 37 years is the most obvious contributor. We cannot separate ourselves from this experience and must look at marriage through the lens of our journey together from courtship, through parenting, and into the empty-nest stage. Like your marriage, ours has negotiated births and deaths, joys and sorrows, stability and transition, comedy and tragedy.
- From our work as marriage and family therapists (for 32 and 21 years), we have learned clinically what can go wrong in a marriage. We know firsthand about those attitudes, behaviors, and patterns of interaction that can sabotage romantic endeavors. We have also witnessed the growth that can be experienced by couples who intentionally work at making

their marriages more creative. Attitudes and behaviors leading to intimacy *can* be developed.

- Teaching marriage and family enrichment courses and leading marriage enrichment retreats sharpen our focus on crisis prevention and making good marriages stronger. Because of the attention given to family dysfunction (neglect, addictions, emotional and physical abuse), our society tends to overlook the good marriages enjoyed by many couples. However, happily married couples offer insight about the characteristics of a stable, happy, even joyful marriage.

- Research and writing in the field of marriage and family is voluminous. When we decided to write this book, we had to decide which themes and issues should be addressed. Over the years we have identified the concepts that couples in therapy and in enrichment events have found most helpful in their journey toward intimacy. These concepts are the ones we include. This research reveals important truths about attitudes and behaviors that contribute to both positive and negative experience in marital relationships. Psychologists have measured what they call "marital satisfaction" and through surveys and interviews identified the factors which are common to couples who score high on these instruments. What issues do happily married couples discuss when asked about their "secrets" for a happy marriage? How do they act? How do they relate differently from other couples? We will combine the results of this research with our own experience as marriage therapists and leaders in marriage enrichment events to discuss the ingredients of life-producing marriages.

- Readers will have to interpret this book in light of their own ethnic background, social history, and religious traditions. We, the authors, are Euro-American, mainline Protestants of the educated middle class. In addition, much of the research on marriage has been conducted by Euro-Americans. We hope that readers of diverse ethnic, socioeconomic, and religious backgrounds will be able to find these concepts useful. But only you can discern whether or not the concepts noted here may be translated into your context.

- Cases from our practice as marriage and family therapists, vignettes from marriage enrichment events, and our own experience as partners will illustrate both the destructive and creative possibilities inherent in the issues we address. Identifying material has been changed to provide anonymity, though the specific dynamics remain intact.

WHAT ABOUT FAITH?

We speak from within the Judeo-Christian tradition and discuss theological concepts that can inform a person's participation in creative marriage. We will discuss how Christian beliefs offer profound concepts and guidelines for creating intimate marital relationships. Many of our choices about what content to include are based on our assumptions about the nature of marriage in the context of the Christian tradition.

- We assume gender equality before God. We believe both women and men are created in God's image, are equally loved and cherished by the Creator, and have the same spiritual, mental, emotional, and relational potential.
- We assume that the ideal Christian marriage is a partnership characterized by mutuality: each spouse is of equal importance, has equal rights, should be treated with equal respect, and has shared responsibility in making decisions and meeting needs of both self and partner.
- We assume that Christian couples are interested in living together with integrity, including a commitment to biblical injunctions about justice. We believe that Christian partners are committed to the words of the prophet Micah, who said, "What does the Lord require of you but to do justice, and to love kindness, and to walk humbly with your God?" (6:8). Treating each other fairly, justly, and righteously is not an easy task, but one to which Christians are committed.

HOW CAN YOU USE THIS BOOK?

We are writing for people who are interested in pursuing both a *theoretical* and an *experiential* understanding of marriage. We offer concepts that can inform and challenge your thinking about the unique relationship called marriage. But we also offer *specific guidance for practicing these ideas*, enabling you to choose new behaviors that can create a more fulfilling, intimate marriage.

We will assume that your marriage is both similar to and different than other marriages. Marriages develop a personality of their own, which we will call a "couple story" in chapter 2. You will identify with much in the following pages, but to get the most from these ideas you will have to translate them directly into the context of your unique marriage.

- Throughout each chapter, we offer exercises that can help you integrate the content. Where these are diagrammed in the text, we include two copies, one for you and one for your spouse. You may choose to stop at those points and apply the ideas discussed to your own marriage through participating in these practical exercises.

- You can participate with your spouse in marriage enrichment groups formed for the purpose of offering support and information to couples who want to strengthen their marriages. Your church or a local counseling center might offer such a group. Many denominations have such programs. Or you could invite other couples in your church to participate in regular sessions to discuss this material.

    The Association of Couples for Marriage Enrichment (ACME) is an organization of couples who are intentional in nurturing their marriages. For information about ACME-sponsored enrichment events and support groups, write ACME at P.O. Box 10596, Winston-Salem, NC 27108, or call (800) 634-8325.

- Suggestions for further reading are provided at the end of each chapter. These materials can help you pursue a particular issue in more depth.

- You can heighten your participation in this process by working with a marriage and family therapist. Consult with a pastor, lawyer, social worker, chaplain, or physician who has been in your geographical location for a long time about a referral to a seasoned, competent counselor. Those certified by the American Association of Pastoral Counselors (9504A Lee Highway, Fairfax, VA 22031-2303; phone [703] 385-6967) or the American Association of Marriage and Family Therapists (1133 15th Street, NW, Suite 300, Washington, DC 20005-2710; phone [202] 452-0109) are among the most skilled in guiding couples into more intimate marriages. Medical insurance may cover such counseling and some counselors work on a sliding fee scale.

- The book is structured so that each chapter can stand on its own. Though many chapters refer back to the skills found in the chapter on communication, any chapter that is of immediate interest to you can be read first. We hope that this book will serve as an ongoing resource. Because you and your partner change, you can continue to use the ideas and exercises as a way of attending to your relationship over the months and years to come.

Now we turn the content of the following chapters over to you, hoping that reading this material will be a worthwhile expenditure of your time and energy. Take care . . . and take action!

one

OVERCOMING LONELINESS
The Journey toward Intimacy

The concept of a journey became meaningful to us, particularly in explaining a seeming contradiction: yes, we *are married*, but we are also in the process of *becoming married*. We began this journey when we met in high school and are still "on the way," a term used by philosopher Gabriel Marcel to describe the human experience of moving into the future. We are on a journey that celebrates the past (where we have been) and anticipates the future (where we are going). Before our wedding we committed to being married. Becoming engaged conveyed to the community our intent to be married. At a specific point in time called "the wedding," we became married, a legal couple with "all the rights and privileges thereof." We know, however, that we are still in the process of becoming married. There is always potential on this journey to reach deeper levels of intimacy as we encounter new experiences brought on by the passing of years and the continuous changes in our life situation.

WHAT IS INTIMACY?

Intimacy, like love, is difficult to define. The word *intimate* means "innermost" and refers to knowing the inner character or essential nature of something. The word refers to a relationship that is closely interconnected. Intimacy occurs when the innermost dimensions of our self (our deepest emotional, spiritual self) are connected to the innermost dimensions of our spouse. An intimate relationship is characterized by a deep friendship and mutual cherishing. *Marital intimacy*, then, can be described as thoroughly knowing and deeply encountering your spouse as a whole person in the context of a committed relationship.

Obviously, intimacy is both inside each partner and between them, because the depth of inner connection expresses itself in outward behaviors. Intimacy cannot be assessed only by external events or physical happenings. Spouses can enjoy dinner together, be compatible tennis partners, or even have a sexual encounter, yet not be experiencing intimacy. Why? Because these events may only represent an external connection between the partners. For intimacy to occur, the connection established must be between our *inner* selves, between the sacred spaces which we might call our "souls." This intimacy establishes a profound relationship with a partner who becomes what Thomas Moore calls, in his book by the same name, our "soul mate."

WHY IS INTIMACY IMPORTANT?

The experience of intimacy is crucial to human existence because it is a major way of meeting the need to belong. This need to belong is as basic as any other need, synonymous with the need to love and be loved. A basic part of our existence as persons is our need to be part of a community, to be in relationship with others, to be important to someone else, and to have a life in the thoughts of another person. Some claim this intimacy need is instinctual because we are born with this desire for contact and connection with other humans. For satisfactory development and maturation, from infancy through the aging process, meeting intimacy needs is as important as food and fluids. A sense of being worthwhile, of having a life with meaning, occurs most fully if we are understood, acknowledged, and cared for by a significant other.

Loneliness is the frightening result of not having this need fulfilled, and some have argued that loneliness is at the root of most emotional problems. Loneliness is experienced as painful and anxiety-producing deprivation. People who seek psychotherapy frequently complain of loneliness and their inability to develop intimate relationships.

The need for intimacy is one of the most powerful motivators of human behavior. One purpose of marriage is to provide a relationship in which we can attain intimacy. The excitement of falling in love is powerful. We feel connected to another person with an invisible bond that promises a degree of fulfillment and satisfaction beyond our dreams.

In the marriage ceremony we hear that "the two shall become one" and are prepared to allow our lives to blend into an entity called marriage. We use the word *intimacy* to describe the profound level of relationship that is possible between marriage partners. From our perspective, intimacy in marriage has potential for contributing to the abundant life that God desires for us.

WHAT DOES THEOLOGY SAY
ABOUT INTIMACY AND LONELINESS?

We know from a psychological perspective the significance of overcoming loneliness. What would theology say about this aspect of the human condition? What does the Judeo-Christian tradition say about loneliness and intimacy? The creation stories from the first two chapters of Genesis offer profound insight into the communal nature of our existence and the need for intimacy.

Created for Community

In the first creation story, as you remember, the earth is finished and all the animals in place when God says, "Let us make humankind in our image, according to our likeness. . . . So God created humankind in his image, in the image of God he created them; male and female he created them" (Gen. 1:26–27). From this significant declaration come several foundational Christian understandings of both the Creator and human nature. Notice the following:

- God said, "Let *us* make . . ." suggesting that somehow God ("us") is by nature in community from the beginning—a truth which the Christian faith tries to grasp and explain through the doctrine of the Trinity.
- Here is the amazing declaration that humans (both male and female) are created in the image of God. We were created purposefully in God's image in order to be in fellowship and communion with God. Why? Because "God is love," says John (1 John 4:8), words which describe a profound truth about the Creator's unconditional love. God desires to establish and maintain a relationship with us. God is not a

loner! God created humans, says the Judeo-Christian tradition, in order to have creatures with whom to relate and to
love.

- Not only were we created for fellowship and communion
  with God, but with each other. One purpose for creating
  male and female was the process of procreation, but beyond
  the vocation of parenting comes something more—an intimacy that reflects our relationship with God. Being completely human, in fact, occurs to the extent that an individual
  is connected to other persons—involved in community.
  Marriage is one context with potential for significant relationship, one opportunity for experiencing intimacy.

Overcoming Loneliness

The second creation story (Gen. 2:4b-25) tells us about the need for
intimacy. It identifies loneliness as the central problem God had to
overcome when creating a bisexual world. As you remember, a male
human is formed out of mud, filled with the breath of life, placed in a
garden, given responsibility for maintaining the garden, and instructed about what fruit to eat. Then there seems to be a pause (after
verse 17), as if God sits back to observe the situation. Suddenly, God
becomes aware that the process of creation is not complete. Something
is not right, something is missing—relationship and community. God
quickly identifies loneliness as the problem and says, "It is not good
that the man should be alone."

Immediately God decides to correct the situation and makes a
promise: "I will make him a helper as his partner" (2:18). So God swings
into action. First God creates the animal kingdom and organizes a pa-
rade of animals. The plan was that the male creature would name the
animals and choose a companion from among them. The man does
name the animals, but (thank goodness!) "there was not found a helper
as his partner" (2:20). God moves to another plan, and we have the famous rib story. God puts the male to sleep, takes one of his ribs, and
carefully forms the woman. When she is brought to the male, he ex-
claims, "This at last is bone of my bone and flesh of my flesh" (2:23). A
"helper as a partner" had finally been found and loneliness overcome.

The story ends by describing that the man and woman "become one flesh." This phrase certainly refers to sexual intercourse, but also defines the possibilities of two persons entering into a relationship that meets the need for intimacy.

The creation stories are clear that humans are created with the need for community. Life as a human person is not complete apart from significant relationships with other persons. We are interdependent creatures, not fully measuring up to our potential without community. This is why God realized during creation that it was "not good that the man should be alone" (2:18), and brought another human into existence: a partner.

Marriage is a particular context in which two persons can give themselves to each other at levels of intimacy that make communion possible. Our capacity to love and create meaning in life can be activated in this context, overcoming loneliness in both parties. Intimacy becomes, therefore, a goal for Christian marriage.

ARE WE AFRAID OF INTIMACY?

This need for intimacy is so strong that it would seem logical that all of us would be moving toward intimacy as quickly as possible—choosing attitudes and behaviors that would offer intimacy to others and invite intimacy from them. In truth, we have some ambivalence about intimacy. To be extremely close to someone can feel threatening. We fear losing our self in the relationship, being smothered or controlled. Assuredly, intimacy makes us vulnerable because we open ourselves in ways that allow a partner to know us more completely than other people. Someone that close can hurt us through ridicule or rejection. We must take risks to overcome these threats in order to be intentional in pursuing intimacy with our partner. The following chapters offer ways of overcoming this fear.

WHAT DOES INTIMACY
IN MARRIAGE LOOK LIKE?

We can define intimacy most effectively by describing what it looks like. What are the beliefs, attitudes, and subsequent actions which characterize those couples who successfully strive toward intimacy? First we will name five characteristics discussed in a later chapter and, therefore, not described in detail here:

Effective Communication: Intimate couples express their thoughts, feelings, hopes, fears, and needs to one another. This mutual sharing expresses a commitment to self-revelation and will be called "knowing and being known" in chapter 3.

Conflict Resolution: Intimate couples accept their anger and conflict, learn how to share these feelings creatively, and are committed to work toward equitable solutions, as we describe in chapter 4.

Shared Power: Intimate couples think of themselves as equals and partners. Chapter 5 will describe the importance of sharing power and authority rather than attempting to control or dominate one another.

Sexual Fulfillment: Sexuality is a primary context for communion. Intimate couples communicate their sexual needs and desires, find time to engage in pleasuring that goes beyond intercourse, and feel mutual fulfillment, as we describe in chapter 6.

Spiritual Connection: Spiritual commitments make significant contributions to the sense of intimacy. Our perceptions about faith, our images of God, and shared religious activity will be discussed in chapter 7.

Other defining characteristics of intimacy are discussed briefly below, but they will surface again in later chapters. We have also described the barriers that can subvert any of these characteristics and disrupt our journey toward intimacy.

Trust

Trust refers to an individual's assured reliance or confident dependence on the character or truth of another person. Trust in marriage means the confident belief in the partner's character, the truth of what is said, the integrity of the self that is disclosed, the honesty of words and deeds, the assurance of a desire to provide for our primary emotional needs, and confidence in the partner's commitment to the relationship. Couples who trust one another experience an emotional security in the relationship. Security establishes a foundation for the openness and freedom that characterize intimacy.

BLESSED is the person whose partner is absolutely trustworthy.

Safety is an important ingredient in trust. This includes the assurance that even in the midst of anger, or during a sexual encounter, we will not hurt one another (as we will discuss more thoroughly in chapters 6 and 7). Marriage can be a sanctuary for partners.

Love offers a sense of security in covenant relationships. This wonderful sense of security comes from trusting that someone else has your best interest in mind, wants to be with you, thinks you are special, and is committed to you. Security is that internal sense that we will survive as a couple whatever threats come our way, either from outside the relationship (employment problems, financial pressure, in-law interference, and so on), or from inside the relationship (conflict, personality differences, unique needs). Commitment (see below) provides security that as individuals and as a couple we will survive the chaos that the rest of life may send our way.

BLESSED are the partners whose marriage provides a sanctuary.

Barriers. Dishonesty, whether about small things or major issues, eats away at trust. Another contributor to mistrust is if either partner worries that during conflict or sexual encounters he or she is not safe, but vulnerable to physical or psychological abuse.

Commitment

Intimacy runs deepest where commitment to the relationship is strong in two ways. First, in a committed marriage partners make the relationship a priority, giving time and energy to making the marriage special. When either spouse is devoted, dedicated, and determined to not only maintain but improve the relationship, then a sense of commitment is felt by both partners. This commitment is expressed through behaviors which communicate that the marriage is a priority. Occasionally one partner sacrifices his or her own needs and desires on behalf of the marriage, which communicates that the marriage is a priority. This level of commitment leads to intimacy.

Second, committed partners assume the long-term nature of the relationship—"till death do us part." They express this assumption in behaviors that link the individual goals of each spouse to the future of the marriage. Partners who look forward to growing old together and plan for the future make psychological and material investments that communicate the desire to be together for the long term. Intimacy is difficult to develop if you suspect that your partner lacks commitment to the future of the relationship.

Most spouses relate commitment to the expectation of faithfulness. Couples who experience the most intimacy feel secure that they are the highest personal priority for their spouse and can expect sexual and emotional fidelity. Words like loyalty and devotion communicate this sense of trust. The threat of affairs is significant in our culture, where work and extracurricular activities provide plenty of opportunities for attraction to another person. Commitment means to intentionally inhibit the amount of attraction, and therefore temptation, to become involved with someone else and sabotage the marriage.

Commitment, then, is an attitude expressed through behaviors that value the relationship and work for its welfare and continuity. Commitment is not just a feeling, but an accomplishment of the will—a choice. Financial investing can be used as a metaphor. Financial advisors suggest that investors deposit a set amount of money on a regular basis regardless of the ups and downs of the stock market. Commitment to marriage is the same. Regardless of whether or not the level of satisfaction, happiness, or closeness is up or down at the moment, we choose to behave in ways that contribute to the overall, long-term growth of the relationship. We invest by working at our communication, resolving conflicts, choosing to have fun, and expressing affirmations, even during periods when our spouse is tired, ill, or preoccupied.

As in financial planning, if over a period of time your emotional investment is providing little return, then a serious evaluation of the relationship is necessary. Why aren't your investments working positively? What is being overlooked? This may be the time to seek professional counseling.

> **Barriers.** When one partner feels in competition for the other's time, attention, and affection with some other person (an affair), or function (like work), or thing (like a hobby), then that partner will feel left out. Security and trust are threatened. Commitment seems compromised. What happens? Dissatisfaction, disillusionment, and distance creep in, allowing estrangement and alienation to dominate.

Openness/Self-disclosure

Intimacy describes a state of relationship in which we can be fully open about who we really are. Intimate partners know and understand each other well. To accomplish this level of openness requires that each partner be willing to be transparent. As we will describe in the chapter on communication, such "knowing" and "being known" calls for significant revelation of thoughts and feelings.

Intimacy cannot be experienced through communication that is limited to the thinking process, but must include emotion (grief, ecstasy, fear, passion, and anger), because emotions are a major ingredient in the human experience. A process of becoming known to each other is discussed in chapter 5.

> **Barriers.** Feeling unknown—or worse, that the partner is barely interested in knowing—makes intimacy almost impossible. When one partner feels the need to be hidden from the other, intimacy is compromised at some basic level. You can't be deeply connected and care for one you don't know.

Acceptance

Intimacy can only happen in the context of acceptance. When a partner is granted access to our innermost thoughts and feelings and really knows our inner self, then acceptance is crucial. To believe that your spouse really knows you "warts and all" and accepts you anyway is a liberating experience and a necessary ingredient in intimacy. This acceptance allows us to be free to explore the deepest corners of our self, knowing that our partner will accept whatever we find.

Acceptance, of course, does not mean tolerating attitudes and behaviors that are unhealthy or destructive to you or the relationship. True love, particularly in a relationship committed to intimacy, is willing to hold the partner accountable for destructive actions—willing to confront irresponsibility and work toward transformation.

> **Barriers.** Any sense of judgment or rejection by a spouse blocks intimacy. Feeling that a part of self is disliked makes it difficult to let any part of the self be known. Likewise, ridicule from either partner makes it difficult to feel intimate. On the other hand, when a spouse's attitude or behavior threatens intimacy, the other partner must confront in order to protect, or lead deeper into, intimacy.

Empathy

Intimacy both results from and contributes to a deep empathy—the willingness to get in our partner's shoes, to "get on each other's wave length." Empathy is not sympathy as in feeling sorry for our spouse. Empathy means the ability and the willingness to try and grasp any life situation in the same way that a spouse does. It is working to see through her or his glasses so that we might understand her or his response. Such empathy allows sharing in the other's hurts, wounds, and pain. Partners who identify with experiences of grief, compassion, anger, joy, and anxiety will be able to provide informed comfort and support. We can feel intimate with a partner whom we feel understands what we are going through.

> **Barriers.** Because our society is immersed in narcissism and focused on personal concerns, partners may not have grown up with a highly developed ability to empathize. Self-centered approaches to life make a person disinterested in the problems or experiences of others. Some spouses may have adopted selfishness as a coping method in their growing up days. It will take work for them to learn to love empathetically.

Affirmation

Affirmation includes recognizing the accomplishments of our spouse at work, in the community, and in the family. We need to communicate what we admire and like about her or him. Affirmation includes expressing appreciation for the ways in which our partner is attending to us and to the relationship. When partners continue to spot each other's strengths, enjoy each other's gifts, and communicate that each is special, intimacy grows. This mutual affirmation meets the need for recognition and appreciation.

EXERCISE: Why Do I Love Thee? Let Me Count the Ways

The following exercise provides an opportunity to intentionally affirm each other. Take a few minutes and think of the "chemistry" that occurred between the two of you during the dating phase. What attracted you to your spouse back then? And what characteristics of your spouse are positive to you in the present?

The second half of the exercise provides an opportunity to see how well you are hearing affirmation from your spouse, or whether your spouse is communicating affirmations. What do you think your spouse was attracted to back then? What is he or she attracted to now?

Write your answers and then find a private time and place to share them verbally with your spouse.

Research on marriage and family stresses the importance of "attachment behaviors"—those small actions which communicate to the partner, "You are special to me" and "You and I have something special going here." Goodbye rituals and "I'm back" greetings, for example, provide a continuous reaffirmation of the relationship and the commitment. The goodbye kiss, the hello hug, the gentle tug on an ear, and other nonerotic touches signal appreciation for the connectedness and pleasure in a unique relationship.

As usual we arrive at a dinner engagement from different places of work in two cars. We finish eating with these friends and head for home in separate cars. As we pull beside each other at a traffic light Judy holds up one finger, then four, then three. In our Lester private

Affirmation Exercise

All of us like to know why our partner chose to marry us and to hear what he or she likes and admires about us. Your spouse would enjoy hearing the same from you. Take a few minutes and list as many specifics as you can in numbers 1 and 2 below.

1. I was really attracted to you when I first met you and during our time of courtship. Here are a few of the many special characteristics that drew me to you then:

2. I *still* love you and am attracted to you. Many of the things mentioned above are still true, but having lived with you for a while, I know you much better and have developed more reasons for loving you. Some of them are:

Now, why do you think your partner was first attracted to you? What do you think he or she likes and respects about you now? List some of these specifics in numbers 3 and 4 below.

3. I am grateful that you married me, but am not always sure why you were attracted to me back then. I will try and identify some of the possibilities:

4. You stay with me so there must be things about me you have grown to like. I'll mention a few:

Affirmation Exercise

All of us like to know why our partner chose to marry us and to hear what he or she likes and admires about us. Your spouse would enjoy hearing the same from you. Take a few minutes and list as many specifics as you can in numbers 1 and 2 below.

1. I was really attracted to you when I first met you and during our time of courtship. Here are a few of the many special characteristics that drew me to you then:

2. I *still* love you and am attracted to you. Many of the things mentioned above are still true, but having lived with you for a while, I know you much better and have developed more reasons for loving you. Some of them are:

Now, why do you think your partner was first attracted to you? What do you think he or she likes and respects about you now? List some of these specifics in numbers 3 and 4 below.

3. I am grateful that you married me, but am not always sure why you were attracted to me back then. I will try and identify some of the possibilities:

4. You stay with me so there must be things about me you have grown to like. I'll mention a few:

ritual talk that means "I (one) love (four) you (three)." Andy responds with the same signal to communicate his mutual feeling.

Barriers. Often our unmet expectations make it difficult to continue this level of excitement and specialness to our beloved. We stop communicating how delighted we are to be in our partner's company and how privileged we feel to share life with her or him. Instead, our anger that he or she is not like we wanted our spouse to be causes us to feel cheated and frustrated with her or him for not measuring up to our ideals. Therefore, we quit communicating our affirmations and begin to whine and complain about our spouse's various shortcomings.

EXERCISE: Identify Your "Love Signals"

Identify the "attachment behaviors," the special little signals by which you and your spouse express your love. If it is hard to recognize any, remember back to your courtship and the early days of marriage. Can you name those that were meaningful then? Assuming that you list several, decide to practice them more intentionally.

If you don't come up with many, resolve to create several small rituals that allow you to express your appreciation and commitment.

Balancing Togetherness with Privacy

Happily married couples find ways to balance a secure sense of connectedness with space for each partner to explore, develop, and express individuality. Connection is fostered by spending time together and by developing a sense of partnership. When a couple is working together on something (parenting, cooking, cleaning, washing) they foster a sense of teamwork. Love is sustained by connection and togetherness, but this love grants each spouse the freedom to develop personal goals, follow individual interests, and express uniqueness in a variety of ways. Emotional space should be granted when a partner needs to be alone. Working out internal thoughts, feelings, or problems may take some private time and space. To have a place of retreat that your partner respects is important.

Intimacy calls for balance between the need for togetherness and the need for apartness, for closeness and distance, for attachment and separation. Partners who bring a mature mix of autonomy (separateness) and homonomy (togetherness) into the relationship, or develop these strengths during the marriage, have a better chance of maintaining this balance. Autonomy is the personal strength to be apart, to be separate, and to trust one's own judgment. It is that inner sense of self that marks one as an individual. The flip side of autonomy is homonomy—the ability to belong to, to be part of, to relate to, and to be intimate with. Most men have been socialized toward autonomy and must work harder to develop homonomy. Women are frequently socialized toward homonomy and may have to struggle to develop autonomy.

> **Barriers.** One danger here is fusion, the suffocating type of togetherness in which two selves are so melded together that each loses personal identity. Fusion may look like intimacy, but it is a forgery because at least one partner's self is lost in the relationship. Intimacy can only occur when two whole selves choose to give to each other. When one self is lost, intimacy and love disappear into codependency. Women are more likely to surrender their autonomy because they are often socialized to feel responsible for making the marriage feel "together." Some men grow up to be dependent on women and are not able to function well unless their spouse is constantly available to respond to their every whim.
>
> At the other extreme is when togetherness is sacrificed on the altar of time-consuming personal interests, busy schedules, or estrangement. This results in living parallel lives. The outcome is a convenient marriage that might be socially acceptable, but in which intimacy does not occur.

Support

In intimate relationships each partner is fully supporting the personal growth of the other vocationally, spiritually, and psychologically. Intimacy is more likely when each partner is "calling out" the gifts of the other and making room in the relationship for the other to express her or his uniqueness. When you feel that your partner desires that you become what you are capable of, your sense of being cared for is deepened. Love grants freedom to others to be who (or what) they feel called to be. Granting freedom is basic to recognizing and caring for a partner, as we shall discuss further around the concept of justice in chapter 7.

Support must be equally expressed toward your partner, your self, and the relationship. During certain periods of time, such as a crisis, support flows mostly in one direction, but in the big picture intimacy depends on a sense of mutuality in the provision of support.

> **Barriers.** Support can become lopsided so that one spouse is in the role of supporter/cheerleader while the other is in the position of needing constant assurance and extra care. This becomes tiresome, and not many are called to spend a marriage as a baby-sitter to the self-esteem of the spouse.

Caring

Intimacy is felt when our spouse looks for ways to care for us. When you feel cared for you feel loved and special, a strong contributor to the sense of intimacy. One acceptable form of competition in marriage is to see who can care for the other more creatively.

In marriage enrichment events and in therapeutic sessions, some spouses ask how to know the difference between caring and codependency. Codependency refers to behavior which covers up, tolerates, excuses, or promotes the destructive behavior of a spouse. Caring, on the other hand, is behavior that meets a real need of a spouse but also expects the spouse to be responsible. In fact, caring leads one to confront behaviors that are destructive. Codependent behavior is not helpful or healthful, but caring behaviors are expressions of love and promote a feeling of intimacy.

Every Christian has responsibility for ministering in the name of Jesus to someone in need. This is particularly true of our spouse. Providing comfort when a spouse is ill, grieved, or upset is a prime example of caregiving. We will, in the apostle Paul's words, "Bear one another's burdens, and in this way . . . fulfill the law of Christ" (Gal.

6:2). As members of the priesthood of believers we extend the care of Christ to others, including our spouse, as we will describe in chapter 7.

> **Barriers.** In our "me first," narcissistic culture, self-centeredness has become a personality characteristic and a way of life for many. In marriage, this selfishness is the opposite of caring. A self-centered person will want to be cared for, to have personal needs met by the spouse, but will have little desire for the giving which is necessary for the act of caring and comforting. Intimacy calls for putting the partner first in certain situations, an attitude that is difficult for the self-centered person.

Affectionate Touch

The giving and receiving of affection through touch is an important contributor to intimacy. Infants satisfy this need through warm and tender touch from caregivers. This physical closeness communicates being connected to another, feeling part of another. Research demonstrates that such touch is necessary for the infant to grow in a healthy way both physically and emotionally. The same is true for marriage. Without affectionate touch, the emotional growth of the relationship, and even the physical health of the partners, is compromised.

Though we grow up learning how to use verbal and visual clues to feel intimate, the meaning of touch never disappears. Those partners who achieve intimacy in their marriage are constantly finding ways to touch one another as a way of communicating their sense of connection and closeness. Partners must search for ways to touch that are comfortable for the spouse. Partners who enjoy touching feel mutual affirmation and communicate their sexual attraction, even though eroticism is not the basic purpose of affectionate touch.

> **Barriers.** One or both partners may have grown up in a family that frowned on touch. Some people grow up without ever seeing affectionate touch between parents. Hugging may have been perceived as inappropriate, too emotional, too demonstrative, or too sexual, leaving the partner who grew up in this circumstance uncomfortable or embarrassed by affectionate touch.
>
> A spouse may have grown up being inappropriately touched and chose to stay clear of any touch in order to try and protect

personal boundaries and feel safe. It is not easy to break out of long-standing patterns, even with a spouse.

Fun and Play

Couples who enjoy each other's company have fun together. They plan time for doing things as partners which they find pleasurable and meaningful. Most couples have fun together during courtship. Intimate couples maintain this ability and desire to play together. Studies reveal that a primary sign of intimacy in a marriage is the enjoyment of play and having fun together. Marriage provides an opportunity for spontaneity, creativity, and joy.

Play is the way children bond with one another. Adult friendships are often built around activities such as bowling leagues, quilting clubs, and dancing classes. Participating in pleasurable activities for fun contributes to a sense of partnership in marriage. Yes, marriage is the context for work and other serious aspects of living, but it is not necessary to live a dull, emotionally dead existence. Nurturing the imagination is essential. Couples who are able to imagine are able to develop exciting and adventuresome activities that enliven the relationship.

EXERCISE: What Do We Enjoy?

With your spouse, make a list of all the activities that you enjoy (from picnics to dancing, from movies to hiking). Beside each activity, note the date that you last participated in this activity. Are you surprised at how long it has been since you last had fun in this way? What keeps you from more frequent play?

Add to this list activities that you have often thought you would like to try. Make plans to have fun this next week, choosing an activity from the list.

> **Barriers.** Some people grow up with such a strong work ethic that they feel irresponsible when they play. Having fun seems to them a luxury in life they cannot afford. They may have grown up in an environment that affirmed work but ridiculed play as lazy, or irresponsible, or unproductive, or something done with idle time. Leaving play out pushes relationships into sterility, lifelessness, and boredom. If you or your partner grew up in this atmosphere you may find it difficult to play and have fun.

Humor

Intimate couples feel free to laugh with each other (not *at* each other). They tease in ways that are affectionate. They laugh over the humorous aspects of their life together. They remember the funny things that have happened and recall them with laughter to celebrate their shared experiences. Teasing and laughing about each others' foibles, of course, can only take place in a relationship already marked by trust so that neither partner has to be defensive or hurt.

> **Barriers.** Some partners grew up in an environment where humor was destructive, focusing on ridicule or extreme teasing that caused loss of self-esteem. They find it difficult to respond positively to humor that seems to raise any criticism. They would also be tempted to use humor as a vehicle for anger. Instead of fun, the purpose of humor would be to express hostility and to hurt a partner.

Time Together

Nurturing our relationship will necessitate spending time together—intimacy doesn't happen in isolation. Communication, sharing, decision making, sexual pleasure, and fun, all take time. Actions and behaviors reflect our priorities. The amount of time you spend together suggests how much you value the relationship. No relationship can be sustained in the face of neglect, indifference, or taking the other for granted.

> One of the most important decisions we (Andy and Judy) made early in marriage was to have a "date night." Friday nights became our date night and we rarely allowed other options to interfere. If something did demand our time on Friday evening, then we rescheduled our date for some other time that weekend.

We want to challenge you to take the "idea" of spending time together and translate it into "do-able" behaviors.

EXERCISE: Spending Quality Time Together

Reflect on the last time you had a date—just the two of you enjoying each other's company, a weekend away without any meetings or responsibilities, or an evening at home without the television. Perhaps it was further in the past than you imagined. Before you go any further in this book, make a date—a time in the near future when you will spend at least two hours together without responsibilities, when each of you is the focus of the other. Plan the what, where, and how so it is on the calendar.

> **Barriers.** Allowing our life situation to control all of our time leads to parallel existence, or a convenience marriage. There are certainly periods of time when circumstances at work, at home, or our health keep us preoccupied. Most of the time, however, not spending time together is the result of choices: either to allow other people to control your schedule (accepting too many responsibilities), or to spend disposable time in other pursuits (TV), or to allow children to come before the marriage in every instance.

GENDER DIFFERENCES

The "battle of the sexes" is so pervasive that coming together in a relationship that reaches levels of intimacy beyond sexual attraction takes intentional commitment. You may despair over the differences between yourself and the one to whom you want to be close, wondering if there is any way to bridge the broad chasm that often seems to separate males and females. Some spouses simply throw up their hands at the idea of ever knowing "what women really want" or "knowing what men really feel." Even if they stay in their present relationship they frequently give up trying to understand the partner and simply accept or tolerate the gap between them. Others become so frustrated with their spouse that they assume these unfathomable differences are specific to this particular partner and leave the relationship for one that they imagine will be "easier to read." We believe these gender differences have the potential to add to the rich mix of intimacy that is possible between males and females. But this calls for intentionally knowing, accepting, and respecting these differences.

From the beliefs about gender mirrored by those around us we develop our own ideas about how males and females feel, think, and act. These differences become ingrained in our worldview along with the values and beliefs described in the next chapter. Some of the most significant differences are related to the experience of intimacy.

Both females and males need intimacy, but generally speaking males must struggle against their socialization more than females to reach this goal. Males are more likely to be socialized toward separation, analysis, rationality, independence, objectivity, and protecting self from external threats. They are usually programmed to deny the emotional self, downplay the need for connectedness, and turn over the caregiving tasks basic to maintaining a loving relationship to women.

In our culture females have been assigned the tasks of relationship, nurturing, and caregiving. Generally speaking, they are socialized to do the work of connecting people, sustaining community, caring for the needs of others, and attending to the emotional side of life. They are focused on attachment, togetherness, and caring. Women often criticize men for being distant, emotionally unavailable, remote, cold, and detached. Those men who are removed from the arena of caregiving—particularly with children, the elderly, and the sick—do not have opportunity to develop caregiving feelings or skills. Therefore, they have a more difficult time developing this side of their personality. How does this work in your marriage?

Many have suggested that this difference in experiencing intimacy plays a major role in most marriage relationships. Women normally need intimacy to feel fulfilled. Men, generally speaking, do not need the same levels of intimacy in order to feel satisfied. Women often expect to experience this level of intimacy in the marriage with the man they love. They often want deeper levels of intimacy than men find comfortable. Some men treat their wife's interest in intimacy as unnecessary, weak, or invasive, and often are made anxious or angry by these "demands." Women historically have had to find this intimacy in their relationships with other women, or sometimes with men who seem (on the surface at least) to be more capable of intimacy than their husbands.

This is not to say that men cannot experience intimacy, but to acknowledge that they have frequently grown up without much instruction or modeling from older males about how intimacy occurs. Our culture's concepts of masculinity and the whole "macho" scene make it difficult for men to feel comfortable with intimate relationships. In fact, some men feel that masculinity and intimacy are opposites. To consider intimacy, therefore, is to risk being unmasculine.

Lance, the son of a former military man, is now a high school football coach. He is the youngest of four and has been smothered and over-protected by his mom. He got a clear message from dad about how men should be tough and independent. He "worked extremely hard to cut loose from mom's tentacles," because of his fear that he was perceived by his father and brothers as "soft." Intimacy is scary to Lance. He seldom initiates touch or any affection with Sara, his wife. To move toward her feels like weakness to him, even though there is a part of him that would like to experience intimacy with Sara. He is consciously having to choose to let go of old messages about how he can relate as a man.

When we pass the romantic illusion period in marriage we must move toward reality in order to have hope. We have much invested in the make-believe partner that we constructed in our minds and hearts. These romantic projections of how he or she would express masculinity or femininity, though grossly unfair, set the stage for disappointment as we move through the stage of disillusionment. We owe it to our spouse to begin the process of moving toward understanding who he or she really is instead of who we imagined and needed her or him to be as male or female.

One of the ways God loves us is by accepting our uniqueness. Though God sees possibilities in all of us, God accepts us for who we are now and loves us fully in our present state, not just because of our future potential. Ideally, we will model after God's unconditional love and work toward loving our partners in the same way: loving them for who they are, not for what we imagined they would be.

THE UNIQUE MEANINGS OF
INTIMACY IN *YOUR* MARRIAGE

The characteristics of intimacy listed earlier can help you assess the levels of intimacy in your own marriage. However, it is important to re-alize that every person has a slightly different perspective about what creates intimacy. It is imperative that the two of you discover your per-sonal perceptions of intimacy. What makes you feel engaged, enhanced, understood, cared for, affirmed, validated, excited, close, and delighted to be married to this wonderful person? You are unique in what you experience as an intimate encounter. You must discover the specifics of what makes you feel intimate. The following exercise can help you track down the specifics of your own experience of intimacy.

EXERCISE: Our Unique Experience of Intimacy

On a piece of paper answer the following questions:

1. Remember three or four special times when you felt quite intimate. Now ask yourself, "What was happening?" Relive the experiences and identify those unique factors that contributed to your feeling of intimacy.
2. What is happening in the present when you feel intimate? Do a little detective work to discover the interactions and behaviors, both verbal and nonverbal, that lead to the feeling. Describe events and interactions which you would perceive to be intimate.
3. When you are not feeling intimate, what is missing?
4. When you read the characteristics of intimacy, which ones are not fully developed in your marriage?
5. What events or behaviors could you and your spouse work together on to create a deeper sense of intimacy?

The next step is to communicate what helps you feel intimate so your partner can choose behaviors which are meaningful to you and enhance your feeling of intimacy. You will find that some of the things that make your partner feel intimate do nothing special for you. Of course the same is true for your spouse, who is wondering why in the world a certain behavior, action, or word makes you feel intimate. What makes her feel cherished might seem odd to you. What makes him feel enhanced and worthwhile might make no sense to you. However, knowing these things allows us to choose behaviors that convey our desire for intimacy.

Achieving an intimate "one flesh" relationship, as we all know experientially, is no easy task. However, couples can be intentional in working toward this level of intimacy. Good marriages don't just happen—they are created by couples who choose attitudes and behaviors that bring intimacy into existence. We hope the following chapters will inform your choices.

IT TAKES TWO

FOR FURTHER READING

Markman, Howard, Scott Stanley, and Susan L. Blumberg. *Fighting for Your Marriage: Positive Steps for Preventing Divorce and Preserving a Lasting Love.* San Francisco: Jossey-Bass Publishers, 1994.
Moore, Thomas. *Soul Mates.* New York: HarperCollins Publishers, 1994.

two
___

THE TWO BECAME ONE
Creating a Couple Story

Aren't you amazed by the differences between yourself and the person you married? Our partners "see" things differently and "do" things differently than we imagined. If spouses came with an instruction booklet, marriages would go more smoothly. Alas, we don't have a manual which describes our partner's idiosyncrasies (idiot-sin-crazies, we think when frustrated). We hear the surprises frequently:

"She doesn't eat breakfast, but she should know that this is the most important meal of the day."

"He always eats all of his vegetables before he touches his meat. Why does he do that?"

"She is always late. Doesn't she know that is irresponsible?"

"He wants *me* to buy birthday cards for *his* family! What's the deal?"

We have no instructions for making sense of our spouse's behavior, no guide to the unique way that he or she understands life, no directions for grasping the oddities of her or his personality. How can we understand what makes our spouse "tick"? How can we grow intimate with someone so different?

SPOUSES COME WITH A STORY

One path to understanding our spouse is to recognize that every person comes with a "story." Knowing your spouse's story can teach you how to understand her or him more completely. It provides insight about how to relate in creative rather than destructive ways.

What do we mean that spouses come with stories? One recent development in psychology called narrative theory offers an excellent understanding of how we develop the unique values, perspectives, and beliefs that shape our attitudes and motivate our behavior. This theory proposes that as we grow up, what we see and hear (all that we experience) is shaped automatically by our mental processes into a story.

As young children we wanted to make sense out of what we saw and heard (also what we touched, tasted, and smelled) so we continually asked the questions "Why?" and "What is that?" As adults we are less vocal but we are always asking inside ourselves, "Why?" "What happened?" "What's going on?" We need an explanation, a way of comprehending what we are seeing and hearing so we can make sense out of our experience and give meaning to life events. So we put pieces of data together in our mind's eye until a story forms, and then we say, "Oh, I see!" In story form the information becomes an event and takes on meaning. Now the things we have seen and heard make sense in the context of our life experience. We can now interpret what happened and even tell this story to others so they can understand.

Our stories provide us with a frame of reference or a worldview. These concepts refer to our understanding of life, the value systems we develop, and the perspective from which we interpret what happens around us. We know that our individual story is influenced by the beliefs and values (including religious views) held by significant people in our environment. While we are children our family bombards us with their ideas about work, play, vacation, religion, money, and so forth. These family narratives develop in the environment of the wider belief systems of the extended family, school system, geographic region, socioeconomic group, and religious tradition, as well as meanings attached to life by gender and ethnic heritage. Through this socialization process, and by adding our own perspectives, we acquire our unique frames of reference about reality, a constantly evolving set of meanings and understandings about life that might be quite different than those of our spouse.

Each of us brings into marriage a story that shapes our perspective on money, sex, discipline, work, and every aspect of married life. Our stories are constructed from thousands upon thousands of observations from which we imagine how males and females should relate as husbands and wives. We construct our unique answers to the question

"What's going on here?" and shape our responses to the world we encounter through the eyes of the life story we are already living. We are constantly interpreting what is going on around us, including the words and actions of our partners. Every word and behavior of our spouse is interpreted from the perspective of our already existing story. This means, of course, that our interpretation of a word or behavior may be miles apart from our spouse's understanding because of the significant differences in our stories, our frames of reference, and therefore our values.

"Where did you get *that* idea?" is a common response to a perspective voiced by our spouse. Deeper levels of intimacy can only be developed by knowing each other's story. Revealing our stories to one another ("knowing and being known" as we call it in chapter 3 when we discuss communication) is the only effective way to communicate who we are to our spouse. Not knowing is dangerous to the health of the marriage and limits the levels of intimacy attainable. We must understand our partner's story in order to grasp her or his perspectives. This makes empathy possible.

MY STORY IS
BETTER THAN YOUR STORY!

We usually learn to believe, either directly or indirectly, that values and behaviors prized by our family and community are better than others'—more correct, more American, or more Christian than competing values and behaviors. Since we want to believe we married someone who is smart, good, and Christian, it disturbs us to discover that our partner holds certain values different than ours. We find out they believe in a different story.

The way people "do life" is passed on to their children. Differences in these life stories can create conflict for partners.

Judy grew up in a family that kept the living room as a "viewing room." It was a place for special guests, to be used only for formal occasions. Part of this was a cultural expectation about how homes should be arranged. Another factor was the necessity of keeping the house nice for potential buyers. Judy's father was a contractor and their house was usually for sale or open as a model.

IT TAKES TWO

Andy's parents, on the other hand, purposefully bought used furniture for the living room so it could double as a play room for the children. There was no other family space for play other than the "living" rooms, so it made sense to use them for play.

However, these reasons were not thought through by either of us. We simply grew up thinking that the way our family did it was the right way, the correct way, the best way. So deciding on how to use a living area was one of our early tasks as a couple. To this day we disagree about the purpose of furniture and how much energy to expend on keeping it looking nice.

Our upbringing also taught stories about the roles which men and women play, particularly in marriage. For some these role assignments are diverse and not gender specific. That is, men and women often do the same chores and share responsibilities for maintaining family life. Others learned a more gender specific view of husband and wife roles.

Judy's father can fix almost anything and routinely did so. Part of Judy's story about marriage was that the husband would fix anything that broke: cars, washing machines, small appliances, and so on. When she asked Andy why the clothes dryer had stopped running, she was shocked that the only thing he knew to do was check to see if it was plugged in and the right buttons pushed. She contained her disappointment, but had to accept a different definition of the masculine role.

EXERCISE: Stories You Brought into the Marriage

The following exercise will allow you to identify some of the stories you and your spouse brought into marriage about values, lifestyle, and role expectations. Fill in the exercise sheet and then use communication skills from chapter 3 to understand how these past stories affect your current relationship.

Arguments can be understood as a conflict between stories. The more diverse the narratives, the more anger and conflict is possible. We will discuss what to do about this anger and conflict in chapter 4.

EXERCISE: Conflict Between Stories

Look back at the previous exercise. Identify how differing values and beliefs create conflict between you and your spouse.

Stories We Brought into the Marriage

Identify several of the particular stories which you and your spouse brought into the marriage relationship.

I. Role expectations for husbands and wives I brought into this relationship:
    1.
    2.
    3.
II. Role expectations for husbands and wives my partner brought into this relationship:
    1.
    2.
    3.
III. Values and beliefs about right and wrong, good and bad, which I brought into this relationship:
    1.
    2.
    3.
IV. Values and beliefs about right and wrong, good and bad, which my partner brought into this relationship:
    1.
    2.
    3.
V. Understandings about how people should "do life" which I brought into this relationship:
    1.
    2.
    3.
VI. Understandings about how people should "do life" which my partner brought into this relationship:
    1.
    2.
    3.

Stories We Brought into the Marriage

Identify several of the particular stories which you and your spouse brought into the marriage relationship.

I. Role expectations for husbands and wives I brought into this relationship:
    1.
    2.
    3.

II. Role expectations for husbands and wives my partner brought into this relationship:
    1.
    2.
    3.

III. Values and beliefs about right and wrong, good and bad, which I brought into this relationship:
    1.
    2.
    3.

IV. Values and beliefs about right and wrong, good and bad, which my partner brought into this relationship:
    1.
    2.
    3.

V. Understandings about how people should "do life" which I brought into this relationship:
    1.
    2.
    3.

VI. Understandings about how people should "do life" which my partner brought into this relationship:
    1.
    2.
    3.

WEAVING A MARITAL STORY

The process of becoming married involves the delicate task of weaving two different, often conflictual stories into a meaningful couple story. The ongoing "I" narratives of both partners must merge into a new and ongoing "we" story. This is another way of describing "becoming one flesh." This "we" story does not replace the "I" stories, but it does express the new identity being established by two people choosing to be in a committed relationship. We must become comfortable weaving "me" with "we." This evolving couple story both incorporates and supports the individual stories of each partner. Because marriage changes the psychological reality of each partner, each partner's present and future story is revised by joining it with the story of a spouse. This couple story provides a strong underpinning for a sense of partnership, of being two people with a special identity. It provides a new context for each partner's future story.

This "we-ness" takes on story form as the two of you develop a perspective that uniquely makes sense out of numerous daily events and interactions. As a couple you create a story about your lives together, including what you value, how you care for each other, and what you are working toward. Creating a story of your life together is one of the primary processes of moving toward intimacy.

Every couple can tell stories about their first meeting, about significant events in their courtship, and about deciding to get married. You and your spouse have many memories of past stories that express the history of your love. One way of nurturing intimacy is telling past stories that demonstrate the commitment and care that characterizes intimacy.

EXERCISE: Remembering the Good Old Days
During one meal a day for one week, take time to remember some of the most important stories about your relationship, those that illustrate how you have woven a couple story. Tell stories about surprises, vacations, parties, special events, meaningful occurrences, crises, times of intimacy, good decisions, and other stories that demonstrate your commitment.

The strength of a marriage is related to our success in forming a mutually satisfying couple story. Narrative theory explains that we are automatically building stories, for better or worse, in every present moment. We have the privilege of self-consciously developing our own couple story: one that is positive, joyful, hopeful, and loving; or one that is negative, dreadful, boring, and ultimately destructive. We can be intentional in shaping stories that represent the excitement and commitment of the relationship, make us feel close and connected, nurture and nourish the marriage, and that we enjoy telling to friends and children.

Some of you are reading this book because you are not satisfied with your current couple story. The marital story is in trouble for one reason or another and the future story is not hopeful. The good news is that you can restructure your marital story, adding different chapters that excite and energize. Like any writing project, you can edit the marital story—changing the plot, the interactions, the characters, and the ending. But we are ahead of ourselves. We need to start at the beginning, the point at which we leave home.

LEAVING HOME:
A NECESSARY JOURNEY

You may be tempted to skip this section if you have been married a long time or are in mid-life. However, if dealing with either set of in-laws is a sore point in your relationship, you might want to read further. Confused, unresolved, or alienated relationships with your parents, siblings, or in-laws can create havoc in a marriage.

Breaking the Ties That Bind

To have a "self" to give in marriage it is necessary for you to experience your "self" as distinct from the family with whom you grew up. This process is called differentiation: distinguishing one's self from that of the parenting figures and separating from the emotional womb of that family. Differentiation is the process of knowing where the boundaries of one's self end and the boundaries of another begin. People who have achieved differentiation are able to participate more completely in intimate relationships without either losing their self in the other, or needing to control the other. Achieving this sense of self is necessary for experiencing your partner as a whole person and giving her or him freedom to be an individual.

Ideally, differentiation is well under way by the wedding and accelerated during the early years of marriage. For many, however, marriage is the litmus test which reveals that differentiation has not proceeded well. Many difficulties in marriage occur because one or both partners were not emotionally ready or able to leave home. Some persons are in mid-life, even involved in a second or third marriage, before finally facing the fact that differentiation has not been accomplished.

> Kurt, who works in an upper level management position, would appear to be differentiated. But before any decisions are made with his wife, Jill, he feels he must first consult with his parents. It seems to Jill that Kurt often gives more weight to his parents' perceptions than he gives to hers. Furthermore, Kurt appears fearful of making a decision if he thinks his parents would disapprove. Jill began to feel that he was much more their son than her husband. She felt like she was in competition with her in-laws. Her frustration with Kurt's dependency led them into therapy.

Why is differentiation important? To be married means taking responsibility for beginning a new family, one that combines the whole self of both partners into an emotional and social entity distinct from their parents. When one spouse's sense of personal identity (individual story) is still encased in the family story of her or his childhood, that spouse doesn't have the freedom to create a new couple story. He or she continues to be committed to the original family's values, philosophy, and lifestyle—unable to assess those beliefs and decide how he or she is different. Under these circumstances commitment to another person or to the development of a new family unit is almost impossible.

We are not talking about leaving home in the sense of rejecting or throwing away your childhood (though some of you come from homes you may want to forget!). You may come from a healthy family whose values you share, whose way of life has integrity you admire, and whose faith you respect. You love the persons in this family and want to stay connected—no problem. Differentiation does not mean giving up love and connection, nor does it mean no longer caring. It does mean choosing to make a primary emotional commitment to the marriage.

In one sense we never completely leave our childhood family. Their ideas, values, and life-styles are deeply ingrained in our personalities. From the back pockets of our minds and hearts, their attitudes can influence us in ways we do not recognize. It becomes important, therefore, to discover what these influences are so we can decide if we want to keep them or change them.

Leaving Mother and Father

We have often said to persons preparing for marriage, "You can only have one 'one-flesh' relationship at a time." Our spouse deserves our primary loyalties, our deepest sharing, and our intense erotic attachments. We cannot give this level of commitment to a spouse, however, until we differentiate from our family of origin. We must leave home by transforming the emotional connections that make parents the priority in life in order to experience intimacy with a spouse. In the excitement of the romantic phase, it seems easy to "leave father and mother" and create a "one flesh" relationship. However, every therapist works with couples whose central problem is rooted in the fact that one or both partners have not yet "left" their mothers, fathers, or other significant adult caregivers.

For some persons, choosing to live and believe differently than their parents seems contradictory to their Christian upbringing, in which they learned to obey father and mother. What are we to do? The Christian faith certainly values family relationships and asks us to honor our father and mother, but it also supports differentiation. For example, the second creation story in Genesis ends with the notation that "a man leaves his father and his mother and clings to his wife, and they become one flesh" (Gen. 2:24). This verse identifies the first step in marriage— becoming emotionally separated from one's family of origin.

Anderson and Fite, in their book *Becoming Married*, point out the paradox of the word "cleave" in older translations of this scripture passage: "leave his father and mother, and *cleave* unto his wife." On the one hand the word *cleave* means "be strongly attached to," in the sense of clinging or sticking tightly to something. On the other hand, *cleave* means the exact opposite, "to sever" or "cut in two," forcing apart two things that were originally connected, or separating something from its source. The truth in these two meanings is that a person must separate from the emotional womb of the family of origin in order to be free to attach to a spouse and create a new womb. Cleaving, in the sense of leaving our original family, must occur before cleaving (establishing intimacy) with a partner is emotionally possible.

From Daughter to Wife and Son to Husband: A Necessary Transition

Another way of describing differentiation is to point out the difficult transition from being primarily a son or daughter to being primarily a husband or wife. One functions differently in these two roles. Many couples are frustrated when one or both behave differently in their parents' homes, or when parents visit, than when they are alone as a couple. Even telephone conversations can have a different tone when parents are on the other end. Often in a marriage enrichment event we ask the couples to describe how each partner is different when around her or his parents. Partners can tell many stories, humorous and not so humorous, about how their spouse changes in the presence of a parent.

Making this transition in identity from child to spouse is crucial to providing space for an intimate marriage. Clues that leaving is not yet finished include the intense need to please parents, functioning primarily to gain their approval, feeling hesitant to do anything without their permission, and worrying about their response to how you are choosing to live your life.

One of the earliest conflicts for many couples is figuring out how to leave home without breaking the connections. A common test comes during the holiday season. More than a few individuals have married assuming that, "Of course we will go to my grandmother's house for Thanksgiving. I always go there," only to find out that the spouse has similar expectations.

There is a sense of loss the first time one cannot be present with the family of origin on special days. The sadness over losing something important, the fear of upsetting parents, and the envy of missing special rituals can make one depressed and frustrated. Sometimes the anger gets expressed toward the spouse: "If I hadn't married you I would be home for Christmas right now!" Instead of blaming, we can care for each other by allowing each to grieve that which has been lost. Then work toward creating holiday rituals that express the couple story that the two of you are weaving.

Parents are also making an adjustment from relating to a child as son or daughter into recognizing him or her as a husband or wife primarily committed to a new identity. For a number of years a couple may face the task of communicating new boundaries of commitment to one or more parents or parent substitutes on either side of the family. The younger the partners when they marry, the more difficulty both children and parents have in making this transition.

BLESSED is the one whose in-laws wholeheartedly
welcome their new daughter or son "in-love."

Differentiation is most difficult when the family of origin resists letting go. Parents or parent surrogates may have perceived your choice of partner, or even your choice to marry, as a rejection.

Elaine's mom was unhappy with her choice to get married. Her mom's behaviors clearly indicated her disapproval of Jamal. She barely acknowledged his presence. Many conversations occurred without any attempt to include him, except for sarcastic comments about his job. Most visits ended with Jamal and Elaine angry with each other due to the tension they felt in her mother's home.

Perhaps your partner's choice to marry you resulted in alienation from her or his family. Consequently you have felt their anger and rejection, feeling unwelcome at family gatherings, and ignored on special occasions. Differentiating without the family's blessing is difficult and sad, though still a psychological and spiritual necessity. Feeling isolated from one's own family or one's in-laws can stress a marriage and complicate completion of the differentiation process. The anger can easily be focused on your spouse, as if he or she was to blame. This is difficult to overcome, and seeking professional consultation may be helpful.

What to Keep and What to Throw Overboard

When couples are moving through the early years of marriage they are deciding, either intentionally or by accident, which aspects of their heritage they want to integrate into this new relationship and which aspects they want to leave behind.

Decisions about what parts of each spouse's family story to integrate into the new couple story can be a major source of conflict. Loyalty to your own family, or simply being content with what you know, can lead you to feel that most of your family tradition must be carried over into the marriage. You may have been brought up in a family in which you felt loved to the degree you adopted and followed the patterns of thinking and acting valued by the family. If you accepted these family values you were considered "good," but if you strayed you were considered "bad." Theologically this leads to idolatry of the family and makes it difficult to leave. You will not feel very comfortable choosing a different life-style, value, or worldview. The fear of rejection by the family of origin is too strong.

Those couples who are intentional about these decisions will avoid some of the conflict. Consider the various stories that you identified in the earlier exercise. Take these values, lifestyles, and role expectations and purposefully develop a couple story about each particular subject.

TIES THAT BIND TOO TIGHTLY

For some of you, leaving mother and father includes escaping from bondage to destructive patterns of living modeled in your family of origin. You grew up in a family that did not function in ways that contributed to your healthy maturation. Your capacities for creating and enjoying intimate relationships, particularly with a spouse, have been stunted. In this sense you are in bondage to patterns of relating and perceptions of marriage that are problematic. As you probably know, the more enmeshed or dysfunctional the family, the more difficult differentiation becomes.

Honor Thy Father and Mother

If you are struggling with a painful separation process, you may use part of the Judeo-Christian story as your excuse. Many persons in therapy have said "the Bible says to honor your father and mother" as an excuse for not choosing differentiation. If your family and religious community stressed this commandment so that it became, without your realizing it, the most important commandment of all, then differentiation is more problematic. As a child you may have identified "honor father and mother" with always being obedient, always making them happy, and always admiring them regardless of their shortcomings. Honor actually means to be faithful in your care and respectful of their perceptions, not blind obedience. Your theological task is to understand this commandment more accurately.

- First, notice that when Jesus was asked, "What is the most important commandment of all?" he did not include "honor thy father and mother" in his answer (Matt. 22:34–40). Rather, he answered that the "greatest and first commandment" is to "love the Lord your God with all your heart, and with all your soul, and with all your mind." Then he added that the second was to "love your neighbor as yourself." A priority of commitments is clearly expressed by Jesus, and it starts with loving God above all else, and then moves to loving others and ourselves. Loving God includes becoming your own self as created in God's image, establishing your own identity, and freely leaving mother and father to become (if you choose) intimately connected with a partner.

- Second, Jesus expanded the concept of family by pointing out that his real family was the community of faith. Remember when his mother and siblings came to where he was teaching and sent word to the front of the crowd that they wanted to visit? In response Jesus asked, "Who are my mother and my brothers?" and then answered, "Whoever does the will of God is my brother and sister and mother" (Mark 3:31–35).

- Third, the first two commandments order us to have no other Gods before Yahweh and not to make any graven images or bow down before them (Exod. 20:2–5). Could it be that you have allowed your parents to be in the center of your life? Is it possible that you are guilty of idolatry because you pay more attention to their desires than to God's?

Liberation from a Dysfunctional Past Story

You may have made strides toward leaving home, but your wounds at the hands of your family are still deep. Your responses to your spouse are still affected by the ways you were abused. For you, leaving mother and father must include escaping from destructive patterns of relating and negative perceptions of marriage. You want to escape "the sins of the parents which are visited unto the children," but find it difficult. Central themes in the gospel can give you the permission, courage, and support necessary.

- First, the Judeo-Christian tradition proclaims that God is always on the side of the oppressed and abused. One of the powerful stories within scripture is the Exodus, the deliverance of the people of Israel from their slavery in Egypt. God desires to deliver us from that which binds us and limits our freedom. The theme of deliverance from captivity is an appropriate analogy to support your move out of your family's patterns and toward intimacy with your marriage partner.
- Second, directly related to this theme of deliverance, is the good news of the gospel about the ministry of Jesus the Christ. In the synagogue at Nazareth he read these words from the prophet Isaiah:

The Spirit of the Lord is upon me,
because he has anointed me to bring good news to the poor.
He has sent me to proclaim release to the captives
and recovery of sight to the blind,
to let the oppressed go free,
to proclaim the year of the Lord's favor.

(Luke 4:18–19)

Jesus' commitment to bring "release to the captives" can provide hope to those who are psychologically bound to their families of origin. His desire "to let the oppressed go free" includes those who have been abused by their caretakers. An appropriate struggle within the Christian journey is to gain freedom from anything that binds us and inhibits our participation in the joys and hopes of intimate marriage.

Survival Stories:
Dangerous to Marital Health

Partners need to identify the coping mechanisms which they learned as children in order to survive in their families of origin. Frequently the coping styles you learned as a child worked; that is, they enabled you to endure and survive your growing up days. Often, however, these same coping styles became part of your ongoing story and are now detrimental to achieving intimacy in marriage. If you can identify these patterns within your story and discover which ones are not working now, you can change. If you do not change these old patterns, you will continue to get wounded in the present.

As a child Anna tried a number of behaviors that she hoped would get attention from her very busy, preoccupied parents. It turned out that screaming and yelling was the most effective in meeting her need for some attention. In her marriage she sometimes feels ignored and uses this same behavior to get Brad's attention. But when Anna screams now, Brad withdraws and shuts down. She feels ignored and insecure. Her behavior does not produce what she needs and wants most from Brad, even though it had worked occasionally with her parents. She had to develop ways to invite Brad's attention and care that were acceptable to him, namely a direct request for his care.

WE KNOW OPPOSITES ATTRACT, BUT THIS IS RIDICULOUS! UNDERSTANDING PERSONALITY DIFFERENCES

Our partner's story includes her or his unique personality. Your partner is "wired" differently: we're not making reference to sexuality here, but discussing how your partner operates in a "different zone" and comes from a "different planet." A mixture of biological and environmental factors (such as family and cultural values) contribute to each partner's personality. The result, of course, is that each of you is uniquely molded and different than the other. These different personalities provide a distinct lens through which each of us views all experience.

Identifying Personality Differences

Couples can become frustrated by their differences. You may see the differences as wrong, mysterious, or unchangeable rather then something that can be understood and changeable. First, we must name and understand these differences. Second, we must learn to appreciate how these characteristics serve the psychological needs of our spouse. Third, we must identify how they affect the relationship.

Ronnie and Rhonda were describing this process in the context of marital therapy. He is extremely verbal, talking fairly constantly when around people. In one marriage enrichment group he was labeled a "talkathon" and asked to monitor his tendency to dominate the process with his words. Rhonda is as quiet as Ronnie is talkative. Rarely does she speak in the group, and then only in response to a direct request for interaction. In their therapeutic process Ronnie learned how talking was his way of compensating for a deep sense of inadequacy, a fear of being ignored, and as the acceptable way to be friendly and therefore to be liked. Rhonda identified how speaking in her family of origin was dangerous. Both parents would "jump on anything you said and make you prove it." Often she felt "made to feel stupid because of what I said." Ridicule was frequent and she learned not to risk being discounted or laughed at by refusing to speak. Being aware of what "talkative" meant to Ronnie and "quiet" to Rhonda, enabled them to develop a deeper empathy. In fact, they made a covenant (see chapter 8) to relate in ways that would more clearly allow Ronnie to claim his personal competence and Rhonda to realize that she did not have to fear ridicule.

We have developed an informal exercise to use in therapy and enrichment events to help couples identify differences in their personalities. This instrument is not scored and has no graphs or charts. It is a conversational piece that enables couples to talk about perceived differences as a way of expanding their awareness. We invite you to pause and participate in this exercise.

EXERCISE: Describing Personality Differences

The following exercise is in the shape of a wheel labeled "Personality Differences." Crossing the center (the axle) are lines, each of which rep-

resents a continuum for a particular personality trait or characteristic.
The words at either end of the line describe the continuum. These
words have been chosen because they are commonly used by couples
in therapy and enrichment events to describe major differences in their
personalities. Please add your own lines with words that describe significant differences between the two of you.

Using your initials, mark on each continuum where you think
your personality fits between the descriptive words at either end.
Then use your partner's initials to mark where you think he or she
fits on that continuum. If you feel that you are much more structured
about life than spontaneous, highly organized and predictable rather
than "loose," then put your initials as far toward the outside of the
circle as matches the strength of your structured self. If your partner
seems opposite, then put her or his initials toward the other end of
the continuum according to the strength of that "unstructured/spon-
taneous" characteristic. For example, Judy and Andy mark this particular continuum as follows:

structured————J—————0—————A———unstructured

This shows that we are quite opposite on this character trait, as we
will describe below.

Let the axle in the center of the wheel represent a balance between
the two characteristics. You may mark your initials close to the middle if you feel your personality is balanced in that area.

Remember, this is not a test. It is an opportunity to identify how
you see yourself and your partner. It can serve as a conversational focus for couples who are looking to increase their understanding of
the relationship. There is no "normal" or "right" or "better" place to
be on the continuum.

After you complete the exercise, compare perceptions. You will have
marked some of the continuums differently. Discuss your definitions
of the words and the meaning each of you gave to that personality
trait. Give specific illustrations of actions and behaviors which led each
of you to put the mark in a specific place on the continuum. Then see if
you can reach a "shared meaning" (see chapter 3 on communication)
about how you conceptualize each other's personality.

We (Judy and Andy) have been helped by noting our significant difference on the continuum that identifies where a person fits around structure and decision making. Andy is at the end of the continuum (unstructured/spontaneous) that identifies someone who likes things open-ended, "loose," and unstructured. He waits to the last minute to make a final decision because he wants maximum flexibility. He considers all the options and wants to make the right decision. Deadlines are not his friends. He may wake up knowing what he needs to accomplish that day, but probably doesn't have a plan or a clear schedule.

Judy is at the other end of the continuum (structured/organized) that says she likes things finished, decided, contained, and structured. She is always planning ahead, making lists, and organizing her schedule. She wakes up on any day knowing exactly what she wants to accomplish with a schedule in place to guide her. She doesn't go to bed until the list is finished. Changes in schedule and interruptions are not her friends. When we understood that both of us want to control our destiny as much as possible, but go at it in different ways, it enabled us to be more supportive of our different ways of doing life.

Why Do Opposites Attract?

We are initially attracted to persons who are different. Why? Some have suggested that we are drawn to characteristics that we admire but which are not fully developed in our own personality. Some psychologists talk about "complementarity," a word describing the process by which a person chooses a marriage partner to assist in strengthening characteristics which are underdeveloped in her or his personality.

Sandra is a very focused, goal-oriented person. She has always been an achiever and thinks of this trait as a strength. Even though she was attracted to Mike, she had difficulty when he would want to kick back and have fun. She has come to appreciate his ability to relax and is letting him help her learn to play.

You may have chosen a partner who has developed traits that are complementary to your own. Within this framework it is possible to think of your personality differences as a positive challenge, to value these differences for what they can teach each of you. To recognize and learn from them expands the growth potential of each partner. A couple

Personality Differences

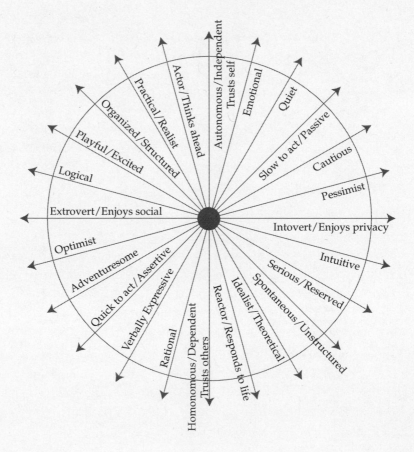

Personality Differences

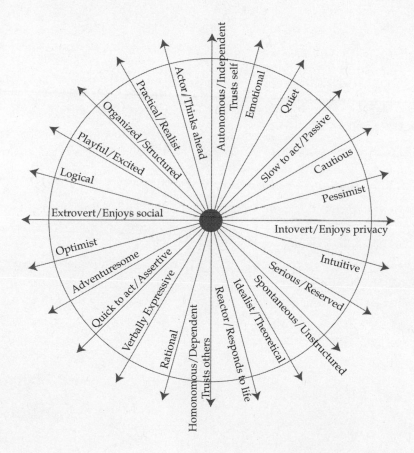

IT TAKES TWO

can gain new insight into their interaction patterns, particularly those that create conflict. As Danny and Angela wrote in a journal entry:

> We are diametrically opposed in the area of personality types. We have used our personal strengths and growing edges to become a very dynamic couple. Putting our types together has resulted in a wholesome and healthy two-part harmony of a marriage. We make a beautiful union of different personalities. . . . We are aware we are different and we are aware that this has been, and still is, an attraction between us.

Personality Characteristics in Conflict

Unfortunately, the personality differences which can be so positive in their complementarity can also drive us nuts! Changing basic personality is difficult, but thank goodness we can change behavior. Couples can identify those behaviors that are extremely irritating to the partner and choose to change or modify them.

Michael, a minister, and Marie, a teacher, illustrate this process. In an enrichment class they completed the Myers-Briggs Type Indicator and realized that he was a strong extrovert and she was a strong introvert. Since they both enjoyed people and were gregarious, they were surprised that she was basically an introvert. This helped them understand a long-standing conflict. The local church Michael pastored had worship services both on Sunday mornings and evenings, making that an emotionally draining day. Given Marie's heavy involvement in the church, both of them were tired by the end of the evening service. Their different desires for what to do after that last service, however, caused continual conflict. As a strong extrovert Michael looked forward to gathering a group of people to head for the nearest pizza place or ice cream parlor. He relaxed and reenergized himself by being around people. Marie, on the other hand, couldn't wait to get home, hop in the bathtub, and read a magazine all by herself. As an introvert she recharged her batteries by being alone.

The conflict came because Michael wanted her to be with him. When he got angry with her for not wanting to go "have fun" with him and the others, he would accuse her of not wanting to support him. She felt unappreciated and unheard because he didn't understand her need for private time after a long day and the need to prepare herself for teaching the next morning. Recognizing and under-standing their differences enabled them to accept the opposite way in which they reenergized themselves. They formed a covenant (see chapter 8) by which they took turns going out and going home. Later they realized that every other week one of them was unhappy and decided they didn't have to be together for that hour after the wor-ship service. They changed the covenant so that he could go relax with a group of people and she could relax privately at home.

Many couples find a rich source of information for understanding both self and each other through various instruments which describe and name personality traits. Behavior patterns of our spouse that seem "weird" or are frustrating suddenly make sense.

EXERCISE: Using Personality Profile Instruments

The use of a self-report personality profile instrument such as the Myers-Briggs Type Indicator (MBTI) will offer another opportunity for understanding your differences and how these differences impact your daily interactions. Find a psychologist, therapist, pastoral coun-selor, chaplain, or other professional who is trained in using person-ality profile instruments such as the MBTI. Many pastors can direct you to such a person. Arrange to take one of these instruments and receive an interpretation. The book by Keirsey and Bates listed at the end of the chapter can lead you through the MBTI.

Gender Differences

Each partner's story is significantly affected by growing up as male or female. Research confirms what wives and husbands know from ex-perience—men and women often see life from different perspectives and live life with different emphases. You already realize that a ro-mantic relationship between a man and woman can be difficult. Even for those couples with the strongest attraction and the deepest com-mitments, understanding each other and meeting each other's needs can be a difficult task.

In our culture men and women have traditionally been assigned dif-ferent personality characteristics as if these characteristics were part of the created order. In reality, character traits assigned to either gender (emotional, logical, assertive, passive, and so forth) are aspects of human personality possible for both genders. Though influenced by both physical inheritance and socialization processes, all character traits can be developed in both men and women. Growing up female or male certainly influences the specific ways in which we think and feel, but this is a cultural variation on the possibilities within creation. Each human is given the privilege and responsibility for developing these characteristics within the limitations of her or his unique individual situation.

Overcoming Conflict by Weaving Differences into the Couple Story

What might our faith contribute to handling these personality differences? First, we can remember that each of us is created in God's image. All of our diverse personality patterns fit under what God called "very good" about creation (Gen. 1:31). We must resist the temptation to identify as "bad" those personality traits of our spouse that irritate us. It is easy to assume that God likes people at *my end* of the continuum better than those people at the *other* end! In fact, there is no ethical superiority at either end. God doesn't favor people who are introverts over extroverts, or people who are structured over those who are unstructured. We can sin at either end of any continuum, or with any personality characteristic.

Second, as believers we have had experience with God's grace. We know that one aspect of this grace is God's acceptance of us with all our human limitations. Acceptance is an important theological concept which describes how we think God chooses to relate to our idiosyncracies. Loving our spouse as God loves us means working toward accepting her or his uniqueness in the same way that God has accepted us. Learn to think of your spouse as different rather than weird, distinct rather than odd.

Third, we can learn to think of complementarity as a gift. By intentionally learning from your spouse how to develop the other end of the personality continuum in your own life, you can become a more well-rounded, balanced individual. In fact, some would argue that a Christian should be working to develop other aspects of self in order to become more mature in life and faith. Expanding the side of your personality that is underdeveloped now can contribute to the intimacy of your marriage.

Fourth, some differences that create stress can be handled by making covenants about changes in behavior that would reduce tension and conflict. Identify these conflictual patterns and use the covenant process (see chapter 8) to change patterns that are irritating. Changing personality is not easy, but changing behavior can be accomplished by willing partners.

INTERRUPTED STORIES

The crises that sooner or later crash into all couple stories can be major threats to intimacy. When a person is facing a trauma, relationships with those he or she loves and lives with are automatically stressed. These experiences must be processed and worked through in order to maintain the emotional and spiritual health of the relationship. Partners must work to protect the relationship from the frustration, depression, anger, or guilt that often accompany crises. Partners who are purposeful in caring for each other during crises will strengthen their bonds.

To protect intimacy, partners must intentionally form a team mentality to deal with the hard knocks of the external world and defend the relationship against crises. How? They keep responses conscious, communicate in-depth about the events, and invite the spouse to participate in thinking and feeling through the loss and change.

Ruben and Isabell believed that their intimacy deepened in the months following the unexpected death of her father. Ruben was able to stay connected by listening to her and holding her during the waves of grief. They talked, she said, for "hour after hour." She was able to trust him with her deep pain, particularly late in the evenings, and his willingness to be present with her made her feel closer than ever.

On the other hand, not handling a crisis creatively can interrupt a relationship or bring it to a grinding halt. If your relationship is "stuck," (you are bored, distant, apathetic, conflicted) do a little detective work and locate the beginning of this "stuckness." Often partners trace the stuckness to a significant change, such as an accident, unemployment, loss of health, or a traumatic loss. Being stuck is a clue that the crisis is not resolved and the unresolved feelings are sabotaging the relationship. Study some literature on recovery from crisis and traumatic experience, or allow a professional to lead you through the process so that you are free to move into the future.

EXERCISE: Evaluate How You Handled a Crisis

With your partner, choose a significant crisis from your past. Evaluate how the two of you handled the crisis.

- How did you relate to one another?
- How well did you understand your different needs (see chapter 8) and offer support?
- What was the effect of this crisis on the level of intimacy that you enjoy? Did it draw you closer, or did it leave some feelings of distance and disappointment (even unresolved anger)?
- If the crisis compromised your sense of intimacy, what could you do to heal the wound to your relationship?
- What could you do differently next time there is a crisis?

One common challenge of marriage partners is how to respond to the change we call "loss." Loss is a basic human experience, one that always affects our close relationships. We know of the high divorce rate that accompanies the loss of a child, for example. Why? Partners rarely grieve in the same manner. Guilt, blame, depression, and "why?" questions almost certainly complicate the grief. In times of loss spouses can consciously choose to share their grief *with* a spouse rather than unconsciously projecting it *onto* their spouse.

Some couples locate a significant loss at the beginning of the marriage, a loss that was symbolized at the wedding.

Sondra left her own faith tradition and joined that of her husband, Jeffrey. She did it willingly because his parents were very upset that he would consider giving up "our church." She underestimated what she would miss in the liturgical tradition she left and did not realize she would have difficulty accepting the more rigid and moralistic standards of his church. Sondra did not feel much loss until the second year of marriage and the birth of twin girls. She was concerned about how to raise them in a tradition where she did not feel comfortable. In the context of a marriage enrichment support group, Sondra shared her sense of loss. Jeffrey had not realized that she was feeling this grief, and was at a point in his own differentiation that he was not trapped by his parents' prejudices. They worked out a covenant that freed her to take the children to events and worship at her former church. They agreed to expose the children to both traditions so they could learn both and as they grew older make their own choice.

Jonathan went against the wishes of his family to marry cross-culturally. His family rejected Juanita from the beginning by refusing to attend the wedding. They sent mail only to him. His invitation to the family Christmas gathering included the suggestion that he come alone, which he refused to do. At first, Jonathan found no problem with the rejection; the chance to separate from his parents had many positive aspects. However, after a few years he felt cut off and began to mourn when his mother was diagnosed with cancer. At first the grief was expressed in anger at Juanita, but he was able to identify his grief and the anger he felt toward his family. Choosing to communicate these feelings with his parents and siblings kept him from blaming Juanita for the estrangement.

Partners in a second marriage may not have finished mourning the loss of a first marriage to death or divorce. The dynamics of grief from death and divorce have some different characteristics, but both demand time to process the loss. Many persons have married too quickly following such a loss and then found that the bereavement process interfered with the creation of a new couple story. For better or worse, they had a couple story with the first partner for which the last chapter had not been finished. The grief process requires slowly "writing" the conclusion to that story so that it becomes history.

CHANGING STORIES

To paraphrase an old bumper sticker—*change happens!* We can always count on change, regardless of how we try to protect against it.

We hope for stability and predictability, but changes in employment, health, finances, world events, religious experience, the health of our parents, and having or not having children put pressure on relationships. We must learn to embrace change and its potential for contributing to intimacy.

Change can be threatening because of its potential to interrupt our comfortable couple story. What if he or she changes her mind about me because of this new job, or living in another city, or this new spiritual quest? A spouse can be in the process of changing but fear communicating the change. What if my spouse is "hurt," or doesn't understand? Will he or she laugh, or ridicule, or ignore, or be threatened, or feel rejected? Change does have the potential to be destructive, of course, but no more so than staying in the same ruts and routines that can lead to boredom.

Fear of change can thwart our attempts at intimacy. Change can threaten a spouse who is stuck in one station on the journey of life. But change is essential to growth; resisting change can stifle growth. We must trust ourselves and our partners in the face of life changes. Anticipation and openness to the future can add spice and vitality to relationships. Flexibility is imperative. Freedom from being locked into the present, not to mention the past, is vital. We must activate our freedom to respond to the realities which are not yet visible, including the potential within our self and in the one to whom we are married.

Love will mature as the years pass, but only if it changes from what it was when we first entered the relationship. Change takes place in our partners. In the fifth, tenth, or twentieth year of marriage we are not married to the same person. Yes, he or she is the same in many ways, but has also changed—physically (balding, weight, health), emotionally (more assertive, more open), and contextually (advancement in a career, changed vocation). Adapting our loving patterns to these changes is basic to continued intimacy.

EXERCISE: Resources for Understanding Changed Stories

Self-report instruments allow a couple to learn more about their different stories and have a guide for discussions that can lead to expanded awareness, increased empathy, and deeper levels of intimacy. Like regular physical checkups, such attention to the relationship allows preventive maintenance. The ENRICH program, for example, provides material for a marital checkup, allowing assessment of change and growth. For referral to a professional who can lead you through this program, write PREPARE/ENRICH, P.O. Box 190, Minneapolis, MN 55440-0190 or call (800) 331-1661. By the way, the PREPARE program helps couples preparing for marriage to evaluate their relationship. New covenants are helpful in meeting changing needs that occur as a relationship moves through the various stages in life (see chapter 8).

Anne Morrow Lindbergh, in her classic *Gift From the Sea*, concludes that "somehow we mistakenly feel that failure to maintain the original pattern of our marriage relationship is tragedy." She notes that many partners feel the change from early patterns of the marriage relationship as a loss and hunger nostalgically for the original pattern of their love. This attitude ignores both the reality and the potentiality of change.

NURTURING HOPE
THROUGH FUTURE STORIES

The couple who experiences happiness, joy, and intimacy is a couple who has hope. Hope is energized by anticipation and expectation about the future. Couple stories that contribute to intimacy, therefore, include a future component that provides hope.

Not only do we have stories of our past which structure the narratives *from* which we live, but it is necessary to create future stories *toward* which we live. At any given moment each of us is working on our "self-in-progress," not only by integrating the past but also by imagining our self into the future. Our sense of personal identity is not only influenced by the past which we remember, but by the future we anticipate. As we imagine ourselves into the future, we develop future stories that are just as important to us as our past and present stories. These future stories make a significant contribution to our identity. We cannot separate who we have been and who we are now from who we imagine we are becoming.

This same dynamic is true for marriage. Couple stories, like individual stories, have a past, a present, and a future. We project ourselves as a married couple into the future by developing stories about the future of the marriage. We not only *are* a married couple, we are *becoming* a married couple, and we give shape to the marriage-in-process through the future stories we create. Couple future stories provide hope for the marriage which in turn provides security, meaning, goals, and dreams.

EXERCISE: Discussing a Future Story

Intentionally set aside one half hour to talk over some aspect of your future that you have not discussed previously. Do this not with the idea of making decisions, but with the goal of exploring all the wonderful possibilities about some future event.

- Perhaps you are a young couple who can discuss your plans for becoming parents. When is the best time? What room will become the nursery? What are some possible names for your children?
- Perhaps you are a mid-life couple who could talk about your retirement. When is the best time to retire? Where will you live? How will you spend your time?
- Other topics could be planning a dream vacation or changing a vocation.

Thinking beyond the "now" is crucial for providing depth and excitement to a marriage. Divergent future stories cause conflict in marriage, so developing future stories to which both partners are committed is an important contribution to intimacy. Keeping specific images of what you want your marriage to become allows you to work specifically toward chosen goals. A couple can be intentional in thinking through coming changes and shape their story to move toward abundant life—to maintain their hope and their intimacy.

Our future stories are rushing at us with new realities and new possibilities. We must leave our narrative open to new plot twists as we move into the future. We must keep in mind that the future will be different in ways that we can't imagine in the present. Knowing the future cannot be predicted should not keep us from imagining the future, but it should keep us from projecting future stories which cannot be amended. Knowing that as a couple we are capable of handling whatever the future brings is an expression of trust in both God's gracious presence and the relationship. We believe in a God who has been with us in the past, is with us in the present, but perhaps most important, we know that God is out in front of us calling us into the future!

FOR FURTHER READING

Anderson, Herbert and Robert C. Fite. *Becoming Married.* Louisville, Ky.: Westminster John Knox Press, 1993.
Keirsey, David and Marilyn Bates. *Please Understand Me.* Del Mar, Calif.: Prometheus Nemesis Books, 1978.

three

THE COMMUNICATION KEY
Sharing and Listening

Who among us has not experienced the frustration of a conversation that went nowhere or that left us feeling misunderstood? Or participated in an interaction that caused hurt feelings and angry frustration? We are amazed that after thirty-seven years of marriage we can still misunderstand one another and have conversations that crash and burn.

INTIMACY AND COMMUNICATION

Overcoming loneliness and establishing intimacy occurs in the context of creative communication. In *The Miracle of Dialogue*, Reuel Howe says, "Dialogue is to love what blood is to the body. When the flow of blood stops the body dies. When dialogue stops, love dies and resentment and hate are born." He speaks of effective communication as miraculous because it "brings relationship into being" and is so powerful that it can even "restore a dead relationship." We have witnessed amazing transformations when couples change their attitudes toward communication and develop new skills.

How do intimate relationships develop? Communication is the bridge which allows partners to form the connectedness in which loving intimacy can happen. Since intimacy involves connection between the innermost parts of each partner's self, then we can only experience intimacy in marriage if we know and are known by each other. How does this knowing and being known happen? First, by choosing to reveal our self. Second, by actively searching for and being available to hear our partner's revelations. Intimate communication is the path into another's inner being, into her or his sacred space. This level of communication, therefore, is potentially sacramental.

Our attitudes toward communication and patterns of conversation are modeled after the people with whom we grew up. These patterns and attitudes may be destructive to intimacy rather than creative of intimacy, but they can be identified and changed. Therefore, this chapter will focus primarily on attitudes toward communication and secondarily on skills.

KNOWING AND BEING KNOWN: SACRAMENTAL COMMUNICATION

Does our faith inform our understanding of the significance of communication? Yes, several concepts within the Christian faith offer encouragement and guidance to Christians who consider entering into intimate communication with a marriage partner. The Christian faith speaks of the possibilities for communicating with God (meditation, prayer, and worship being the most obvious). We suggest that the process of attaining spiritual depth can serve as a model for attaining intimacy within a marriage.

Self-Disclosure and Intimacy

We can only know God to the degree that God initiates through self-disclosure. Relating to God intimately would not be possible if God had not decided to become known. One of Job's friends said, "Can you find out the deep things of God? Can you find out the limit of the Almighty?" (Job 11:7). The answer, of course, is no—not unless God chooses to make these "deep things" known. If God chose to stay hidden, we would not know of divine love and grace nor experience redemption, healing, and forgiveness. Marriage partners can only know each other to the degree that they are willing to "open up." Our partners cannot know the "deep things" about us unless we choose to be known.

When God initiates communication, we call this knowledge revelation—a word that literally means "to unveil, to disclose something that was hidden." To reach intimacy, communication must occur at a significantly different level than everyday conversations. Marriage partners can choose to "unveil" themselves to one another, making themselves more fully known.

Christians have always believed that our knowledge of God through revelation came as a gift, freely imparted by a gracious creator. In marriage, intimate knowledge about our self is also a gift, freely given because we want to be known at a deeper level.

> BLESSED is the spouse whose partner chooses
> to be "unveiled" in the marriage.

What is revealed? God gives more than ideas and information; God offers communion. Revelation is not impersonal, but is an intimate encounter with God and with God's deeper concerns and desires for the creation. Communication between spouses, if intimacy is to occur, must include more than surface observations. It must reveal deeper dreams, anxieties, and hopes—those dynamics of life that invite intimacy.

The Nature of Love

But why did God choose to become known to us? Christians believe that love is the primary defining characteristic of God and that this love motivated God to bring the creation, and specifically human beings, into existence. Why? Love, by its very nature, desires intimate relationship. Since intimacy is only possible where persons know each other, God's love seeks to know and make itself known to those created in God's image for the purpose of communion. If love motivated God's revelation, then our love should express itself in our desire to know and be known by our partner.

The Importance of Self-Awareness

If we want to be known to our partner we must be willing to develop our own self-awareness. Anytime one partner grows in self-understanding and is willing to reveal this new awareness, the potential for intimacy is increased. Obviously the reverse is also true: to the degree that an individual is out of touch with her or his interior self, intimacy is limited. A spouse can choose to enrich a marriage by embarking on a process of self understanding, followed by the willingness to communicate this new self-awareness to the spouse.

Through a course at school, Samuel became aware of sexual abuse he had experienced as a child. He came into therapy to learn more about himself. This helped him understand his anxiety and strong desire to be alone when he watched similar experiences on the news or in the movies. Furthermore, he was finding it difficult to feel comfortable touching his infant son whether changing a diaper or feeding him. When he shared these new understandings with Patty they felt a deeper sense of intimacy.

> BLESSED is the spouse whose partner desires
> an increase in self-awareness.

Partners who want to move to a new level of intimacy will choose to search themselves until they know what they really think and feel, and then communicate the truth of these discoveries to their partner.

Intimacy and Being Known

Not only has God chosen to become known to us, but we believe that we are known by God. The words of Psalm 139 express the connection between being known by God and intimacy with God as felt by the psalmist:

> O Lord, you have searched me and known me. You know when I sit down and when I rise up; you discern my thoughts from far away. You search out my path and my lying down, and are acquainted with all my ways. Even before a word is on my tongue, O Lord, you know it completely. . . . Such knowledge is too wonderful for me; it is so high that I cannot attain it. (Psalm 139:1–6)

This overwhelming awareness that God knows us so completely both comes from and leads to meaningful divine/human encounters. A person who feels God's involvement at this level usually has a deep sense of connectedness with God. Truly, experiencing God's desire to know us makes us more willing to share ourselves in prayer and worship.

Similarly, in marriage, a sense of intimacy is related to how well a person feels known by her or his partner. When you can say that your partner has "searched me" and "discern[ed] my thoughts," you feel intimate with her or him.

> BLESSED is the person whose partner wants to
> "search out my path . . . and [be] acquainted with all my ways."

To feel that your spouse is "acquainted with all my ways," and to realize that he or she still loves you, can lead to a profound sense of awe.

Behavioral and Verbal Sources of Revelation

Revelation is occurring constantly between partners. We are continuously interpreting our spouse's body language, actions, silences, facial expressions, and use of time and energy. This behavioral revelation is a significant window into a partner's story, but is not sufficient as a full introduction to thoughts, feelings, and values. We can only know our partner's deepest motivations and concerns through the spoken word.

> If Andy goes to the garage and backs the car out into the driveway while I am finishing getting ready to go, it is easy for me, Judy, to make assumptions on the basis of my growing up. I can interpret his behavior to mean, "I'm in a hurry; it will be your fault if we are late!" or "I'm ready and I am angry that you aren't!" Only through his spoken words can I learn that he went out early to start the air conditioner and begin cooling down the car. Behavior wasn't clear; only by asking for and receiving verbal communication could I clarify that he is caring for me rather than making a demand or expressing an accusation.

Unless we choose to make the "deeper things" about our self known, our partner can only operate on the less certain (and sometimes misperceived) impressions received through our actions.

The Mystery of Self

You may be saying to yourself, "But God is not fully known to us." True, but that is the nature of all persons. Our inner space, our complete story, cannot be fully known either to ourselves or to another person. In this sense each of us remains to some degree an unfathomable mystery, which partners can trust and respect. Communication of our self, therefore, can never be complete, even though we continue to dig deeper.

The good news is that every communication remains filled with potential; it is never finished or exhausted. Every word or phrase we use has the potential for deeper meaning. There is depth to our spouse that we can continue to search out, and a depth to our self that we can choose to discover and make known. Complete intimacy is never achieved, but is a goal we pursue over the years by inviting our spouse ever deeper into the sacred places of our mind and heart.

When we desire to know and be known by our partner, we trust that God's Spirit is working within us and between us to facilitate new depths of understanding. Since "we do not know how to pray as we ought," the apostle Paul informs us in Romans, "the Spirit helps us in our weakness" and "intercedes with sighs too deep for words" (8:26). He goes on to say, "God, who searches the heart, knows what is the mind of the Spirit," a testimony to God's desire to know our thoughts and feelings, even those not clearly known to us. The same Spirit intercedes between us as husbands and wives when thoughts and feelings are not yet named, not yet conscious, not yet speakable. Invite God's presence, trust the Spirit, and be receptive.

ETHICAL CRITERIA
FOR COMMUNICATION

Communication can lead to intimacy and even bring healing to broken relationships. But communication can also be used for the opposite purpose, to conceal rather than reveal, to close rather than open, to lie rather than speak the truth. This unethical use of language leads to alienation rather than intimacy. Christian love, therefore, demands that certain ethical criteria serve as a basic commitment for communication with our spouse.

Revealing Rather Than Hiding or Withholding

One meaning of sin is to refuse to acknowledge God's love, to resist God's invitation to participate in a loving relationship. We can sin against our spouse by withdrawing from communication—depriving her or him of connection with our inner self. We can make our self known in personal encounters, or we can choose to hide or distort ourselves—which effectively blocks intimacy.

BLESSED is the spouse whose partner is secure with "openness."

When a spouse hides much of her or his self and refuses to become known, the partner feels lonely and abandoned. As the lonely partner's hunger for intimacy grows, he or she will be more likely to eroticize another relationship, particularly one in which self-revelation does occur and deeper levels of intimacy become possible.

Warren came into therapy in order to "do something different" about his marriage. What caused him to realize that the marriage was not what he wanted? He found himself day-dreaming about other women, not so much in erotic or sexual images (contrary to gender stereotypes), but with fantasies about intimate conversations in which he could just talk. Warren and his wife, Robin, seldom shared any thoughts or feelings with each other, primarily because of his fear of criticism and her fear of conflict. He decided to take the risk of revealing more about himself to Robin. She was pleased with his initiatives and began to take risks to share more of herself. They moved slowly but meaningfully into more intimate communication.

Honesty Rather Than Falsehood

Basic honesty is a major contributor to trust. The injunction in Ephesians to "put away falsehood" and "speak the truth" (4:25) identifies one way in which those committed to following Jesus the Christ "do life" differently. When we misrepresent ourselves, we are functioning dishonestly and making a mockery out of communication.

Jackie married six months ago. She feels sure that her husband loves her, but she has found him to be untruthful on several occasions. She reports being "on edge and suspicious" of him. She is constantly wondering if what he says is truthful, or whether he is hiding or misrepresenting something. One disturbing consequence of this response is that she holds back from giving herself to the relationship as fully as she wants. The result, of course, is that instead of moving toward intimacy they are becoming more distant and alienated.

Being intimate with someone who is dishonest is impossible.

Jesus said, "You will know the truth, and the truth will make you free" (John 8:32). Communication makes knowing truth about the other possible and makes us free to enter intimate relationships. But a partner who is frightened, or feels vulnerable, or is trying to control will be tempted to use communication to distort or falsify the truth, to misrepresent reality.

BLESSED is the spouse whose partner is honest and speaks the truth.

Clarity Rather Than Confusion

The scriptures teach that God is not the author of confusion. We must take seriously Jesus' words about letting our "yes" mean yes and our "no" mean no as described in Matthew 5:37. If we follow this model, our conversations should consist of simple and direct statements. Within marriage we have responsibility to communicate in ways that clarify, making it easy for our spouse to interpret.

When the apostle Paul is critiquing the practice of speaking in tongues, he points out that if flutes and harps "do not give distinct notes, how will anyone know what is being played?" (1 Cor. 14:7). Using a military analogy, Paul says that a trumpet must blow clearly for the troops to understand the orders. Hints and innuendoes are usually not helpful. Our partner is not responsible for reading our mind. Partners need to say it straight and keep messages congruent.

BLESSED is the spouse whose partner is committed
to achieving clear understanding in conversation.

Why is clarity important? Paul explains further in 1 Corinthians 14:8–11. Verse 11 says, "If then I do not know the meaning of a sound, I will be a foreigner to the speaker and the speaker a foreigner to me." When spouses use language to confuse, distort, or hide, they will be strangers to one another, making intimacy impossible.

Mutuality Rather Than Control

Communication has consensus as its goal rather than control by one spouse over the other. A partner will invite new perspectives but will not attempt to impose her or his way of seeing things onto the other. Communication will take place with constant respect for the partner's perspective. Manipulation or exploitation are not the purposes of communication between marriage partners.

> Warren's wife, Robin, was too alienated to come, so he came to therapy by himself (as we mentioned earlier). He was dissatisfied with the distance between he and his wife and the increasing conflict between them. One of Warren's most important discoveries was that he always tried to make Robin feel like he wanted her to feel. When he asked how she felt about something, and her response was not what he thought it should be, he would proceed to tell her how she should respond. Robin, of course, would become angry, get quiet, and withdraw. She wanted her perception of feelings and needs to be respected. She told Warren that she was smart enough to know her own thoughts and feelings. He finally realized, "No wonder I didn't understand why she always says, 'I just can't win.'" He began inviting her to share herself and then listened to her perceptions with acceptance and respect.

We will describe the principle of mutuality and partnership that God intended for marital relationships in chapter 5.

THE CONTEXT FOR
INTIMATE COMMUNICATION

Self-disclosure is not an easy task. We live in a culture that often demands our real self be hidden—sometimes even misrepresented. We must be concerned with "appropriate" content and "acceptable" tone in order to negotiate daily existence in the workplace, neighborhood, church, and even the extended family. When someone asks, "How are you?" we are not able to answer fully. Issues of trust and confidentiality are not clear. We are always measuring to what degree we can be vulnerable to another person.

Marriage, however, has the potential for more complete disclosure of ourselves. It can be a safe place where our deepest joys, griefs, fears, and dreams can be shared without anxiety. For a marriage to become such a sanctuary a certain context must be established.

Trust

To make our inner selves known is to be vulnerable. How will my partner respond to these parts of myself that I have shared? We must trust that our partner will treat our revelations with tenderness and respect. If you suspect that your spouse might respond with ridicule, judgment, or rejection, you will either be superficial, distort the truth, or stop talking altogether in order to protect yourself. Feeling unsafe is one reason why a partner erects invisible walls within the marriage.

Bob and Susan decided to visit a marriage counselor to try and understand why they were feeling so distant after only eleven months of marriage. They uncovered an important event. Bob, a very sensitive man, grew up with a macho model of being closed about one's feelings. He held his emotions in check. When he married he imagined being more open with Susan. On their honeymoon he teared up during a movie. She became uncomfortable and, not knowing how to respond, she laughed. He described his response as being embarrassed, exposed, and ridiculed. As a result he "shut down." Now they are working in therapy to establish more open communication. Bob is attempting to trust her not to make fun of his emotional self. Susan learned that she did not communicate her desire to know Bob more intimately. She is now inviting him to share himself and affirming his disclosures.

Development of this trust is particularly necessary when trust has been violated in the past by a parent or significant other.

BLESSED is the spouse whose partner is completely trustworthy.

Confidentiality

What will my partner do with this knowledge about my self now in her or his possession? We must be able to trust that our spouse will maintain the boundaries which we need to extend around the partnership. By boundary we mean the invisible protective curtain that is erected around a particular relationship to provide a context of privacy and security. We must be able to assume that this relationship has priority over others. We must trust that our partner will not reveal our inner self or the dynamics of the relationship to someone outside without permission. We must be certain that he or she will not expose us.

Establishing these boundaries is not always easy because different partners have different perceptions about appropriate boundaries for confidentiality.

> Barry described how careful he was about sharing his thoughts with his wife, Connie, because she "immediately picks up the phone to tell one of her sisters or her best friend." Barry was a more "private" person, he said, and it made him feel "naked" when Connie told other people what he was thinking or feeling. Connie said that it was important for her "to share her feelings with people who would understand and sympathize" with her. She didn't have any sense of embarrassment about letting their life together be an "open book" to her sisters and her best friends. It became clear to her that his fear of exposure became a prime reason for the lack of intimacy that she craved. Over several weeks she resisted his need, but finally agreed that she would respect his boundaries by reporting to others only *her* inner self and not Barry's. She agreed that she would ask what aspects of his inner self and their life together he felt should be private and which she could share with others. This decision allowed Barry to be more open with Connie and contributed to deeper levels of intimacy.

Notice the gender differences here. Like many males, Barry shares fewer of his inner thoughts and feelings with friends, particularly those feelings that make him feel vulnerable. Connie, like many females, feels free to share many of her thoughts and feelings with those to whom she feels close.

Desire to Know

We must be confident that our partner really wants to know our story more fully, yearning for a deeper knowledge of our self. Most of us assume that if a partner loves us, he or she will be interested in the story we have to share. If we doubt our partner's desire to know us, we will hide ourselves rather than seek to be known. Likewise, we must communicate interest in our partner's inner self by finding ways to invite sharing—to demonstrate verbally and nonverbally that we want to know more of her or his story.

Careful Listening

If our partner is listening carefully, and we know that we are being taken seriously, it allows us to share deeper thoughts and feelings. On the other hand, if our partner seems bored, or gives the message that sharing is a waste of time, or communicates that we should hurry up and finish, then we don't feel the freedom to go deeper. Careful, disciplined, empathic listening is a major contributor to intimacy. This is why revelation rarely occurs when the TV is on, or when one is also reading or involved in some other activity. One of the rarest of gifts within a marriage is when each spouse listens to the other's story with such careful and focused attention that each feels completely heard.

Time and Patience

We need assurance that a partner will take the time necessary to hear our revelations. Full disclosure takes time for most of us, not five minutes before leaving for work or going to bed. Why does revealing who I am at a given moment take time? I might not have identified clearly for myself what I am thinking or feeling about a particular event. For example, if one of us asks the other, "What did you think about the movie (or book, or accident, or news, or the play)?" the responder might not yet be ready to talk. Emotions may be running high and thoughts jumbled in a complex mix. To begin a response takes a moment, perhaps hours or days, of reflection. Even then the response may proceed slowly as the partner attempts to conceptualize and then find the right words. Couples seeking intimacy commit the time it takes for each partner to identify and communicate thoughts and feelings.

BLESSED is the spouse whose partner takes time to listen carefully.

These couples will also be intentional about coming together again for further sharing. At dinner the next evening the question will be broached again, "What further thoughts have you had about the movie (book, accident, news, play)?" Sharing our response to a life situation is like the preparation of a speech; it takes several drafts. An intimate partner is one who takes time to hear each draft, and then takes the last draft more seriously than the first.

EXERCISE: Explore Your Context for Intimate Conversations
Discuss with each other these ideas about the basic ingredients necessary for intimate conversation (trust, confidentiality, desire to know, careful listening, and time and patience). Which of them do you do best? Which of them can you work on to enable more intimate communication? Develop a plan for changing behavior for changing the context (see chapter 8 for guidance on making covenants).

THE FEAR OF BEING KNOWN

But suppose all of these factors are present and you are still fearful. Perhaps you know that you don't communicate clearly and that you resist revealing yourself to your partner. Why can't you be revealing, clear, and honest? For some reason you expect conversation will be painful, conflictual, frustrating, or embarrassing, so you turn on the TV, stay at work, go to bed early, focus on the children, or read the newspaper rather than take the risk. What is going on? Would you like to understand your reluctance, that fear which quickly blocks any attempt to express yourself at a deeper level? It might help to explore your previous experiences with self-disclosure.

Is it possible that every time you attempted to express yourself as a child, conflict seemed to erupt? When you expressed a need or an opinion did people respond with ridicule? Did you grow up with family and friends who laughed at your ideas and feelings, taunting you as if you were stupid or ignorant? Were you judged harshly or even rejected when you described your feelings? Did you experience betrayal at the hands of a family member, a friend, or a previous mate? When you made yourself known to another person did he or she choose to use this knowledge to hurt you? Did you feel exposed, embarrassed, or uncomfortably vulnerable in a previous relationship when you let that person know your real feelings and thoughts? If the answer to any of these questions is yes, then you learned in childhood, or later in a significant relationship, that letting your inner soul be known was too risky.

> Oliver was so deeply wounded both as a child and in his first marriage that he has great difficulty allowing himself to be vulnerable with his new wife. He tends to hide himself for fear that he will be picked on and ridiculed. A major issue in therapy is his work toward healing these old wounds and learning that Darlene was more trustworthy—that she wanted him to feel good about himself, not to hurt him. They joined a marriage enrichment group that met regularly, where Oliver learned from watching other couples that it could be safe to be open within a trusting relationship.

The fact is that when we make ourselves known, we become vulnerable to ridicule, disagreement, rejection, accusations, and the resulting conflict. This is why trust is so important. But the bottom line is still the truth: without revealing your real self, without taking the risk of becoming known, intimacy is impossible. Perhaps with the theological concepts stated earlier, and a renewed trust in your partner, you can take a step toward being known. Spending time with a counselor might allow you to overcome this fear.

GENDER DIFFERENCES

Given the different ways in which men and women are socialized, it is not surprising that we use conversation for different purposes and express ourselves with different patterns. After all, communication is our way of interacting with the world. When the world models for us that certain behaviors and styles are appropriate for our gender, then our communication patterns will reflect those models. Some authors suggest that the meanings and purposes of communication for males and females are so different that conversation between them can be compared with any other cross-cultural experience.

We must be careful not to think that these patterns of communication are "natural" or biologically based. Many males communicate in ways that are more common for females and vice versa. When we describe gender differences in marriage enrichment courses, most couples confirm that their communication patterns fit many gender specific characteristics. However, most couples can also illustrate how their patterns are different: the husband communicating with characteristics which are normative for women and the wife communicating with characteristic patterns more frequently associated with men. As you read the differences described below, notice to what extent they fit you and your spouse. Your specific upbringing and experience will probably have programmed you toward some communication patterns associated with the other gender.

Women's Communication: Purposes and Patterns

Women value equality and connection, so it is not surprising that the primary purpose of communication for most women is to establish, develop, and nurture relationships. Through conversation women express support, experience closeness, and strengthen the bonds of connection. Some specific characteristics of female conversation are:

Supportive. Most women are socialized to be caregivers and to take responsibility for enabling others to feel good. It is not surprising that they use communication to offer support, to express sympathy, and to encourage others. They often respond with comments such as, "I have felt that way myself, I know how you feel." Women's patterns of communication have been described as responsive because they are able to respond to what others say in ways that make the other person feel important and valued ("That is amazing," or "I'm so excited for you," or "I can't imagine how you could stand it").

Cooperative. Women are often socialized to function more cooperatively than competitively. Their conversation is more inviting, making room for others to join in and express their own feelings and thoughts without having to disagree or become competitive with an idea already expressed. Women in conversation with each other rarely argue; rather, they continue to share various perceptions without feeling the need to "win over" the others to a particular point of view.

Participatory. One feature of women's communication is their tendency to speak in ways that invite participation from others. They often qualify a comment with a disclaimer ("I'm not sure, but I think . . . ") or attach a question at the end of a statement ("I think it is time to replace the refrigerator, what do you think?"). Identifying with the other person's experience in a give-and-take style allows the participants to feel equal and connected.

Emotive. Compared to men, women are not as afraid of emotions. They more freely share at feeling levels about life situations they are confronting. Women usually assume that relationships are enhanced when emotional responses to life are included in the conversation. Sharing of feelings also allows identification with the other person and strengthens the sense that "we are all in this together." Emotional sharing increases the connection between women and furthers the sense of closeness and friendship.

Men's Communication:
Purposes and Patterns

Most men live in a world which has taught them to value independence over dependence or interdependence; to desire being in control over being controlled; to achieve status (being higher, better, more successful) as a primary goal; and to function competitively rather than cooperatively in achieving independence, control, and status. Therefore, masculine communication patterns often serve these values and objectives.

Independent. Men may use conversation to maintain independence. This makes it difficult to invite participation because participation suggests interdependence. They tend to state their ideas as final

IT TAKES TWO

rather than tentative, rarely inviting response or critique. Men can be supportive, but usually in a manner that does not invade the privacy of the other person. Their conversation does not usually invite the other parties to share. Men are more likely to make statements than ask questions. They tend to give orders and tell others what to do or think.

In Control. Being in control makes it difficult for men to use conversation in a way that invites cooperation. Men usually feel more free to use conversation in ways that offer advice, suggest ways to fix something, or communicate knowledge. A man is more likely to communicate in an argumentative style in order to "win" the other person to his point of view.

Status Conscious. Men compete through conversation when they are debating points of view, telling information, and arguing about the relative merits of their perceptions. If a man is trying to gain status in a conversation, he must exhibit more knowledge or superior arguing skills. Masculine conversation patterns are more likely to be assertive in expressing opinions.

Nonemotive. Men are less likely to communicate a broad range of feelings. Fearing vulnerability or ridicule, they are hesitant to share feelings of tenderness, uncertainty, passion, or sadness. They are more free to communicate aggressive emotions.

Conflict in Purpose and Process

Given the differences in the purposes and patterns of conversation between males and females, it is no wonder that having productive conversations is so difficult. Conversations between a husband and wife can be like trying to cross a mine field; the dangers are unmarked and can explode at any moment. Identifying potential hazards to your conversational health can start with the following map of the mine field.

What's Wrong, Honey?

Males and females often show support in different ways. Conversation for men is a means to an end. Men usually show support by trying to help, but their way of helping is by trying to fix it—so they tend to offer advice. When men discuss a problem, it is normal for other males to offer suggestions and solutions.

For women conversation is a process that in itself is meaningful. Women show support by identifying with the speaker's problem or concern—so they offer sympathetic responses that acknowledge feelings and confirm the other person's expression of concern. When women describe a problem they are not necessarily asking for answers or wanting someone to fix it; they are looking to make connections with someone who understands and can empathize.

When a wife has a concern, she is more likely to share it with her husband, particularly if he has been sensitive enough to ask, "What's wrong, honey?" Even if she does say, "Oh, nothing," she is probably inviting more initiative from him. When she does share what is happening, she will want sympathetic listening and confirmation that he understands her concern—which is what she would receive from her female friends. But given his masculine upbringing, he will probably offer suggestions about how she can fix the problem that is causing her concern.

She may respond with resistance, even anger, to his "how to fix it" suggestions, interpreting that he is unconcerned and insensitive. He, of course, thinks she shared the concern because she needed advice. In the masculine world you don't share problems unless you want help. Since he thinks he is being helpful, he doesn't understand her disappointment. When she doesn't follow his advice he may feel unappreciated.

Most men are raised with primary emphasis on being strong, which includes being self-sufficient. Asking for help is considered being "wimpy." When men are faced with a problem, therefore, they frequently do not want to talk about it for fear of feeling ashamed of themselves, or being perceived by others as dependent and needy. When she says, "What's wrong, honey? You are awfully quiet tonight," he will likely say, "Nothing." This, when translated, means, "Nothing I can't handle by myself, and if I talk with you about it I will feel weak and that will add to my sense of vulnerability." His male friends understand this interpretation and don't follow up with another question. They simply move on to politics or sports.

However, since she values being connected she may express support by pushing further ("It will help if you talk" or "Come on, I know something is bothering you"). To her female friends this would feel like concern, an invitation to further conversation. But to him it may feel invasive. He may respond with anger that she is pushing toward his vulnerability ("I said, nothing is wrong!"). Now she will feel hurt and pushed away rather than included, while he may feel angry at her invasion and guilty that he has somehow hurt her. This leads to either more distance and silence or to further conflict as they express their anger, fear, and hurt by arguing over other things.

"Get to the Point!" versus "What Else Happened?"

Another difference in male and female communication patterns has to do with detail. Men tend to tell a story from start to finish and include less detail. Women are more likely to include substories and more details, particularly about the people involved. The details men include are more likely to be impersonal and informational, while the details included by women are more likely to be personal and interpretive. A man might tell the story about a friend's new job and include information about the nature of the work but not about his friend's feelings. In fact, how his friend felt probably was peripheral to the conversation. When a woman hears a friend talk about a new job, the friend's feelings would be a primary agenda. If she told the story to her husband she would automatically include her interpretation of her friend's feelings.

Men are amazed that female friends who haven't seen each other in a while can spend a weekend catching up on their personal lives while they (males) only need an hour to catch up on personal issues with male friends before turning to external agendas like work and finance.

I (Andy) recently had an opportunity to spend a day with our son when we were both in Chicago on the same weekend. We intentionally arrived early and spent the day together. Since he had begun a special relationship with a woman we had not met, Judy asked me to find out more about her. So I asked Scott about this relationship, knowing it was more special than previous ones. He shared some information about who she was and how they met, but not much about his feelings. Of course, I didn't ask that question. When I returned home and finished telling Judy what little I knew, she asked with surprise, "You mean you spent the day with Scott, and that's all you know?"

The Significance of Emotion

Intimacy in marriage progresses only as deeply as the quality of shared feelings allows. Many men find it difficult to express tender, affectionate emotion. They probably grew up seeing few male role models expressing gentle, caring, nurturing feelings. It is also difficult to express emotions that make them feel weak and vulnerable—such as fear, doubt, anxiety, and shame. Such emotions in men are frowned upon by many in our culture because toughness and aggression are prized. He may be afraid to express such emotion for fear that it makes him appear weak and unmanly.

This fear can be a major block to communication in marriage—to knowing and being known. Since tender emotions are threatening, the male will often function in ways that attempt to keep these positive emotions out of the relationship.

> Mark was one of four boys. Being strong and showing no emotion were valued characteristics in his family. He does not allow his wife, Nanette, to see his vulnerable side. When he lost his job to downsizing, he refused to share his anxiety with her, even when he began to have physical symptoms of stress. Furthermore, he gets threatened when Nanette is upset. When she expressed her anxiety about his unemployment and his physical symptoms, he refused to listen. Mark thinks that crying is a weakness. When Nanette cries he demands that she stop immediately. If she doesn't "cut it off" he threatens to leave the room. Over several months a marriage enrichment group helped him reevaluate his negative thoughts about emotion and he was willing to begin sharing more of his "weaker" emotions.

If a man devalues emotion and thinks of it as dangerous, he will not want to be aware of his own emotions, much less let them be known to his partner. When you grow up with macho models for inhibiting emotion, anything but hardness and aggression are difficult to recognize, much less share.

"Honey, Would You Mind . . . ?"

When a women asks a man to do something that gives him status and recognizes his distinctiveness ("Honey, would you move those heavy chairs into the dining room?") it is easy for him to respond positively. If she asks him to do something that she or someone else in the family could do ("Honey, would you call and see what time mother's plane arrives?") he might be more resistive and irritated. Why the problem? Because down deep he may feel that he has been told what to do, thus experiencing a loss of status and independence. If he does make the call to the airline, their responses may be quite opposite. She believes that he has chosen to share life with her and feels cared for, while he may feel put down and mildly irritated. He may resist calling the airport because "nobody tells me what to do" and be satisfied that he has protected his independence, while she would feel hurt that he doesn't care enough to help.

Even more problematic is when the wife asks the husband to do something that he thinks is not a manly task ("Honey, would you make Sara's sandwich?" or "Charlie, Eloise needs her diaper changed."). His internal response may be that he has a lot of status to lose doing a task that he feels women should do. It might be difficult for him to respond affirmatively without feeling that he is giving up his independence.

This dynamic explains why a wife who makes a simple request can be thought of as "bossy" while a husband who makes a straightforward request is perceived as "direct." In our culture men are given the privilege of being direct. Women, however, may be penalized by men who feel that a female who is direct is "ordering him around."

> Early in our marriage I (Judy) would ask Andy, "Where would you like to go for dinner Friday night?" Even though I wanted to go to a particular restaurant, I felt that to tell him my desire would be too assertive. I wanted him to engage in a give-and-take discussion until my desire could be made known. Then I hoped he would pick up on my preference and agree to go to the place I had chosen. However, as a man, Andy heard my question as an invitation to decide, so he would make a decision and think he had responded in a way that was pleasing to me. Of course, I felt unheard and my desires ignored.

The double jeopardy, of course, is that men then criticize women for not being "straight" with their communication ("Why didn't you just say that?").

Decision Making

Another example of this independence versus connection difference shows up in decision making. If consultation with his wife feels like a loss of independence, the husband will tend to make decisions without consulting her. He may even assume, without realizing it, that he is the one who knows best and thinks through things more carefully. She will feel left out rather than included as a partner, and he will not understand her hurt.

William grew up with a dominating mother who constantly demanded of him. In his marriage he often left Barbara out of the decision-making process. The event that brought them to a counselor was when he bought a car without consulting her. He did not understand her anger at first, but finally "heard" her sense of being "left out" and treated "as if I am dumb." He identified that his behavior was largely related to his fear that "she would take over like mom." He feared losing his autonomy if he included Barbara in his process.

Women tend to consult, assuming that a consensus can be reached so that no one person has to make the decision. Men are more likely to make their suggestions and then assume that the one with the most status will decide. Women may hesitate to make their preferences known lest they be thought of as pushy, while if men do not express an opinion they may be perceived as powerless.

Becoming Bilingual:
The Path toward Intimacy

Partners must consider these differences if they are to understand the reasons behind difficult communication. Some answers to the male question, "What does she really want?" and the female question, "Why is he so insensitive?" are found in comprehending the purposes behind what men and women say and also what they hear.

Recognizing that the differences are related to socialization processes, and not inherently better or worse, allows both partners to respect both modes. You may have learned to value one style and devalue another. Biology is not destiny, so patterns of behavior that result from our training as males and females can be modified. Each partner has the ability to expand her or his portfolio of communication styles. Each can learn not only how to hear the other, but how to use other patterns of conversation to increase understanding.

BLESSED is the spouse whose partner wants to learn
her or his patterns of communication.

The more trapped you are in your gender's style of communication, the more difficulty you will experience in trying to communicate creatively with your spouse. Only partners who become bilingual, who learn to use and understand the patterns of both genders, have the potential to reach the levels of understanding necessary for intimacy.

EXERCISE: Which Gender Patterns Describe You?

Discuss with your spouse the traditional differences in patterns of communication between genders described above and address the following questions:

1. How do these patterns fit the two of you?
2. What are the differences?
3. What could you do to become more bilingual and understand more completely each other's patterns of communication?

If you would like to pursue this whole idea more thoroughly you might read Tannen's book mentioned at the end of the chapter.

COMMUNICATION SKILLS

Doesn't communication come naturally? Can't we just talk? No, communication patterns are learned behavior. You learned patterns of speech and attitudes toward communication, both helpful and not so helpful, both from the people with whom you grew up and the surrounding culture. These patterns and attitudes contribute to breakdowns in communication with your spouse. Couples who come for counseling often present their problem as, "We can't communicate!" They usually mean, "We don't understand each other."

To communicate well, we must overcome the differences in the way we see and understand what happens around us. As we mentioned in the last chapter, we all interpret life differently. From our unique histories and personalities we create stories about the world that influence how we interpret events. You and your spouse will see the same situation differently, even having different perceptions of what actually happened. Then you will interpret the situation differently on the basis of your distinct values, beliefs, and worldviews. Each of you also has different needs, desires, and expectations. In short, the same situation can be understood by each of you from completely different perspectives.

Though both verbal and nonverbal communication are important, we will focus on conversation—the spoken word. Communication theorists have learned many concepts and skills that enable more effective conversation patterns between partners. The theorists who have developed the Couples Communication program (Sherod Miller, Daniel Wackman, Elam Nunnally, and Phyllis Miller) have been in the forefront of research and writing on communication. Below we discuss two concepts from their book *Connecting* (see "For Further Reading" at the end of the chapter) that are helpful to couples seeking deeper experiences of intimacy.

Awareness Wheel

Misunderstanding between partners often results because one partner is not aware of or misinterprets a thought, feeling, need, or intention that is basic to the other partner's response to a situation. When our communication patterns hinder us from communicating thoroughly, our partner reacts to a message which is not complete. So we say to one another, "Where did you get that idea?" or, "What on earth were you thinking about?" or, "Why did you do that?" Communication goes best when we enter a time of mutual gathering of information. In *Connecting* the authors further develop a concept called the "Awareness Wheel" that directs each partner to address five dimensions of self when communicating about a particular issue.

Data. What are the facts? We are constantly taking in information through our senses, particularly with our eyes and ears, that influence what we think and feel. Our partner needs to know what we saw and heard that led to our thinking, feeling, and acting. We each have that "sixth sense" called intuition that reflects the insight, hunches, memories, and associations from our previous experiences (our personal story). When communicating with our partner, it is important to include this data.

Thoughts. Thinking includes the analytical, logical, and rational process by which we interpret and make sense of the information. Our thoughts are formed by our interpretations of the sensory data, our existing beliefs—those values and meanings which we already possess and which influence our interpretation of any situation, and our expectations for the future—what we anticipate will happen next. Our thoughts can be expressed as opinions, ideas, assumptions, and judgments.

Feelings. Feelings are the emotional responses we have to a situation. They may be pleasant (happy, sexy, satisfied, excited, pleased, romantic, delighted) or unpleasant (anxious, angry, depressed, sad, disappointed, embarrassed, lonely, fearful). Feelings are themselves important information which influence and are influenced by our thoughts and actions. Because many people in our culture are suspicious of emotion, it is easy to let feelings go unnoticed or unexpressed. Our partners will usually sense the feelings anyway, but their history may lead them to ignore or misinterpret the important emotional component of our message. To make communication complete, identifying feelings is important.

Wants. Wants are what we desire for ourselves, our spouse, and the relationship. Wants include the physical, social, and psychological needs which we hope our relationship will meet. Words such as intentions, desires, dreams, hopes, goals, and objectives communicate the human drive to move toward the future. Wants reflect things we want to be (happy, healthy, affirmed), to do (read, finish a task, change jobs), and to have (a financial plan, a vacation, a better relationship).

Actions. Actions are what we do, how we behave. Actions can be past (what we have already done at some previous time), present (what we are currently doing), and future (what we plan to do). Actions which are future oriented are particularly important to enriching a marriage. In the arena of future actions are the choices for changing behaviors which inhibit intimacy and adopting behaviors that lead to more intimacy. Letting your partner know what you plan to do next is an important part of complete communication.

When discussing an important issue, partners can intentionally include each dimension of the awareness wheel in their communication. These five dimensions provide guidance in sharing as completely as possible the various facets of our response to the issue at hand. The sending partner can speak from each dimension and, when finished, can ask if any dimension has been left out by asking, "What else do you need to know to make sense of all this?" The listening partner can assist by asking for information from any dimension, "I hear your thoughts, but I'm not sure about your feelings," or "I understand that you are frustrated, but I'm not sure of the data to which you are responding. Can you fill in the blanks?" As mentioned earlier, the content of each dimension may change or expand as each partner deepens self-awareness about her or his experience of this event.

EXERCISE: Practicing the Awareness Wheel

Choose an important issue with which one or both of you are now involved (a decision you are considering, a problem with a child or an aging parent, a situation in the workplace or at church, a philosophical or theological question, or another issue of importance to you). Take time to sit with each other in a quiet environment at home (no TV!), in a park or a restaurant, and purposefully share as much as you can with each other about your response to the issue using each dimension of the awareness wheel.

When you finish, ask these two questions: What did you learn that was unknown until this conversation? How does this knowledge change things between you?

This process might feel stilted or artificial until you get used to it, but hopefully you will have fun exploring a more intentional way of understanding each other. I (Judy) ask clients to think back to when they were learning how to drive a car and recall the amount of energy that had to be focused on each part of the process which they now do automatically.

Because of our unique personality and communication styles, each partner will tend to start with or emphasize one or two dimensions of the awareness wheel. Likewise, each partner will tend to overlook or discount several dimensions.

Roy will usually start with his interpretation and analysis before reporting the observations which led to the interpretation. Next he normally moves to a statement of intentions, but rarely expresses his feelings unless his wife thinks to ask.

Cheryl tends to act first—slamming the door, making a phone call, finding information from the *TV Guide*, getting dressed, putting on a particular piece of music—before her husband knows her intentions. He won't know what she is thinking or feeling unless he asks.

Jonathan frequently expresses his emotions quickly and moves to his intentions or actions before it is clear to his partner what data he is responding to or how he interprets this data.

Where a partner starts on the awareness wheel is not important as long as he or she eventually addresses all five dimensions. Problems occur when we use only one or two dimensions of the awareness wheel and ignore the others, leaving our partner unsure where we are coming from and where we are going in our response to a given situation.

Many interactions ("Pass the salt, please") do not call for this degree of intentionality and thoroughness. At times, however, you need to ask your partner for an "appointment," signaling that you need some specific time with her or him to communicate more completely about a situation.

Shared Meanings

The second significant concept in communication is the process of making sure that we are talking about the same thing. A common occurrence in marriage therapy is when a couple in conflict suddenly realizes, with the help of the therapist, that they are misunderstanding what each other was trying to say. Since our worldviews are so different (because of our gender, upbringing, personality, and so forth), it is easy to jump to conclusions about our partner's thoughts or feelings. That is, we "hear" a meaning, an implication, an accusation, a feeling, or a decision that is not accurate. We fill in the blank with our own perceptions and projections. When a misunderstanding takes place, the rest of the communication is skewed because the partners are in essence talking about two different things.

Every communication theory includes a feedback process, or what *Connecting* calls reaching a "shared meaning." First the receiver of a message summarizes what he or she has heard (including data, thoughts, feelings, intentions, and perhaps actions). Then the partner who sent the message can check the summary for accuracy. If the partner who sent the message feels accurately heard, then he or she can continue. However, if he or she feels that the message was not heard fully, or accurately, then he or she can send the message again, or correct the misunderstanding, or expand the message so that the point is made more clearly.

Either partner can initiate. If you are the receiving partner you can say something like, "Let me make sure I am understanding you. I think you are telling me that . . . ," and then offer a summary in your own words. The temptation is to interpret or evaluate what has been heard, but that will skew the process. Or the partner who is sending the message can stop and ask the listening partner to summarize what has been heard: "I've said enough; would you tell me what you have heard to this point?"

When the message has been confirmed then the listener can offer the gift of validation to her or his partner. Validation could be simply saying, "It makes sense that you would feel that way" or "Now I understand what you are thinking." Validation of feelings, even when we disagree, leads to intimacy.

Taking time to clarify allows the couple to stay on the same wavelength and reduce the interference in their communication. At every step in the communication process a couple checks to make sure they have the same understanding of the message being sent. Knowing that a partner is working hard at hearing exactly what you want to say leads to a sense of intimacy.

We cannot have a creative dialogue unless we understand what the other is experiencing, called empathy. Empathy is not agreement, but the willingness to listen thoroughly enough to "hear" one's mate so that we know better what he or she is thinking and feeling. We know where our spouse is coming from, whether we agree with his or her conclusions or not. Intimate communication is characterized by both partners wanting to be known to the other. Each partner is attempting to fully understand what the conversation is meaning to the other.

OTHER WAYS OF COMMUNICATING

Conversation is basic, but there are other ways of communicating important thoughts and ideas to your partner.

Letters

Writing a letter to a spouse might seem like a lot of work when you could simply speak your mind. After all, aren't letters more impersonal than personal communication? Not necessarily. Before telephones, writing letters was an art form which could be very personal. If you have read the collected letters of a famous person, or the private diaries of almost anyone, you will see how deeply personal the written word can be. By writing your spouse you can choose to express yourself more thoroughly through carefully selected words and sentences about a significant theme or concern. Both thoughts and emotions, intentions and actions, can be carefully conveyed in this manner. Your spouse can read your full account and digest for hours or days before responding. Then you can have conversation with your written word as the agenda.

Other Writings

You may find in books, magazines, or the newspaper, ideas that express your perceptions. They may express feelings about concepts and concerns that are more complete than you could easily speak. Pointing these out to your spouse and inviting her or him to read a certain article or chapter can be a significant way of sharing yourself. Of course, this is most intimate when followed by conversation around the ideas and feelings expressed in the written word. Some partners have taken a spouse to a movie or a play that communicates something important about themselves or the relationship, again to open up a conversation.

Intimate communication is hard work. The process that leads toward deeper levels of knowing and being known can lead to unexpected conflict. If this occurs, don't give up. We will offer help in dealing with conflict in chapter 4.

FOR FURTHER READING

Gray, John. *Men Are From Mars, Women Are From Venus.* New York: Harper Collins, 1992.

Miller, Sherod, Daniel Wackman, Elam Nunnally, and Phyllis A. Miller. *Connecting: With Self and Others.* Littleton, Colo.: Interpersonal Communication Programs, Inc., 1992.

Nichols, Michael P. *The Lost Art of Listening.* New York: The Guilford Press, 1995.

Tannen, Deborah. *You Just Don't Understand.* New York: William Morrow and Company, Inc., 1990.

four

MURDER, THEY WROTE!
Confronting Anger and Conflict

The anger which surfaced was by far our biggest surprise in the first years of marriage. We believed that loving each other would protect us from anger toward one another. We avoided serious conflict during our courtship. We assumed that the "perfect love" we pledged at our wedding would send us through a life of bliss filled with romantic feelings toward each other. Ha! Such was our naiveté. Like all other couples, of course, we found that those warm fuzzy feelings of affection could turn into the cold scratchy feelings of resentment and disappointment.

Even more problematic was the fact that we had no clue how to handle this anger creatively. We both came into the marriage committed not to express loud, abusive anger. We did not want to hurt each other. With no family models for handling anger creatively, however, we handled it poorly. Having vowed not to express anger through yelling and fighting, we handled it indirectly through silence and withdrawal, which still caused pain.

> I (Judy) could get quiet in a way that made it clear that I had "quit talking for a reason and you better find out what it is!" My silence could be cut with a knife. I (Andy) withdrew, not only from conversation, but literally choosing somewhere else to go—usually the library where I found it impossible to study, since my stomach was in a knot and I was furious inside. Or I went to the gym where I could express anger vicariously through playing basketball.

Our actions resulted in both physical and emotional distance, with estrangement the consequence. Obviously, we could not maintain a sense of intimacy during those experiences.

Not only were we surprised by anger, and incapable of handling it creatively, we were also frightened by it. Given our experience growing up we knew that anger could result in being out of control, hurtful language, alienation, violence, and other destructive behavior. Judy was threatened by the possibility of judgment, rejection, abandonment, and loss of security. Andy was threatened by the loss of approval and the sense of inadequacy to make everything normal again. Furthermore, both of us were frightened by our interpretation that the anger, and the resulting alienation, meant that we did not love each other and shouldn't have gotten married. We assumed that anger was bad, an expression of hate instead of love, which meant to us that we were in trouble.

Our problem, obviously, was avoiding and even denying our anger. We overcontrolled this emotion. Some of you struggle with the opposite problem—expressing anger too quickly and harshly. You undercontrol your anger, lashing out in hurtful words and actions. You may be concerned about the emotional pain caused by hot flashes of caustic speech and personal attack. In either case, handling anger more creatively is a key to intimate marital relationships.

MARRIAGE AND CONFLICT

We learned the hard way what may be obvious to most readers: no intimate relationship can exist without conflict. Regardless of how much you love your spouse, how well you communicate, how carefully you meet each other's needs, and how similar your personalities, conflict will occur. Love cannot escape anger! Surely Adam and Eve were mumbling their anger toward each other as they left the Garden of Eden, arguing about who was to blame for the fiasco.

Adam: (accusingly) Now look what you've done, you got us kicked out of the garden.
Eve: (defensively) How could I know the snake was deceiving me?
Adam: (blaming) You should have known it was a trick.
Eve: (sarcastically) If you're so smart why did you take a bite? You can't fool me; you were trying to gain knowledge of good and evil for yourself.

Adam: (defensively) I was not! If you had explained what the snake
said more clearly, I wouldn't have been fooled.

Eve: (caustically) The Lord didn't seem too impressed with your
excuses.

And so it goes through the ages. When two persons with different personalities and different histories bring a variety of life experiences, values, and worldviews into a close relationship, there is bound to be
conflict. No two people see the world in the same way, have the same
needs, nor value the same way of "doing" life. Nothing can protect us
from disappointment, change, stress, and other dynamics that create
conflict. As marriage partners our choice is not whether to have anger
and conflict but how maturely and creatively we will handle it. This
chapter offers ideas that will enable you to reduce the amount of conflict and handle what remains more creatively.

Anger Can Be Destructive

Hans Selye says in *The Stress of Life* that many people in our culture
die from what he calls "wear and tear diseases." We would say that
anger, particularly unresolved or chronic anger, is a "wear and tear disease" to the healthy marriage. Anger can make a marriage painful and
shorten the life span of the relationship. Marital wars (either cold or
hot) interrupt intimacy for long periods of time during which a marriage can be "worn down" in ways that are difficult to repair. The author of Ephesians names some of the results of anger that is not
resolved, including bitterness, wrangling, slander, and malice (4:31).

David Mace says, "The failure to achieve love and intimacy is almost
always due to the inability of the persons concerned to deal creatively
with anger." The inability to deal with anger creatively is a major reason relationships fail to achieve a deeper level of intimacy. Anger that
goes unresolved, or has been handled in a manner that seems insensitive or unjust to one partner, will become a barrier to intimacy. Preventing anger from becoming destructive is one of the most important
keys to achieving intimacy in marriage.

But Anger Can Lead to Intimacy

Conflict can be a vehicle of growth rather than the hammer which
destroys a marriage. Love and anger are not contradictory! Anger can

be viewed as an opportunity for growth. Anger signals that pain is present and needs attention. More specifically, an "anger event" can serve as a "diagnostic window" through which a couple can gain new insight into both themselves and the relationship. Identifying threats (which we will describe below) reveals knowledge that leads both the individual and the couple into expanded self-awareness.

We learned that working together as partners to negotiate a resolution to anger is one way of expressing love, care, and commitment. Willingness to learn new insights in the context of a conflict opens the door toward deeper levels of intimacy. Placing an experience of anger on the table communicates that the marriage is a priority and we want to immediately face anything that threatens to reduce the intimacy.

If you grew up being told that any expression of anger is bad, sinful, rude, immature, irrational, and/or unchristian, you may find it difficult to consider anger as a contributor to intimacy. If you learned that anger was something "good people" should ignore until it goes away, then you will have difficulty in capturing anger's potential for intimacy.

When we married we believed deep in our hearts that if we were to openly acknowledge and express our anger that our marriage would be in jeopardy. We were amazed that no catastrophe occurred when we finally took the risk of expressing our anger straightforwardly. To our surprise and delight, we reached a new level of respect and intimacy we didn't know existed. We were excited at the expanded freedom to discuss any subject without censoring those issues or perspectives we feared would create tension and conflict. We reached a deeper level of honesty.

> BLESSED is the spouse whose partner is committed
> to dealing openly and honestly with angry feelings.

Effective ways of coping with anger and conflict are necessary for a couple who desires an intimate marriage. To move in a creative direction demands a willingness to grasp what anger is and where it comes from. Intimate couples make a commitment to move toward resolution and reconciliation in the present and prevention in the future.

WHY DO WE GET ANGRY?

If someone had asked Adam why he was angry, he might have answered, "Because Eve got us kicked out of the garden." Eve might have answered, "Because Adam ate the fruit too, but he's blaming me for the problem." An easy first response when angry is to blame our spouse's words or actions, to assume that he or she made us angry. Really understanding anger, of course, calls for a deeper search. The questions Where does anger come from? and Why do people get angry? have intrigued observers of the human situation for centuries. What is happening when we feel tense anger welling up within us; when our teeth clench, our jaw tightens, and our stomach knots up; when suddenly we shout upstairs, "Can't you ever get ready on time?"; or when we pivot and leave in a huff?

Social scientists, particularly psychologists, have developed a variety of perspectives on the issues of anger and interpersonal conflict. One common thread runs through all these interpretations and explanations: anger occurs when a person feels threatened. We get angry because we feel threatened by some person or some life situation. We have interpreted some action, word, or event as dangerous. We imagine that physically, socially, or psychologically our self is being threatened. A basic value, belief, or expectation seems to be under attack.

Melissa strongly believed that couples should share all of their feelings with each other. Her high expectation in her new marriage was that she and Brandon would talk for hours about their various experiences and what was going on in their lives. He was quiet during their brief courtship, but she had anticipated an increase in freedom to share after they were actually married. Two years into the marriage they came into counseling because of the anger and bitterness she felt toward him for not communicating in the relationship. She interpreted that "his silence means he doesn't love me enough to want to talk and share with me!" The anger surfaced in response to the threat she felt to her value of sharing and her fear that the marriage was in jeopardy.

Any threat perceived by the self triggers an internal alarm system indicating that we are under attack. In response to this "call to arms" our whole being automatically goes "on alert," mobilizing in response to the perceived danger. This arousal pattern is a complex series of body changes that include rising blood pressure, rapid heartbeat, tensed muscles, increased perspiration, and a change in blood chemistry. In one of our most primitive physiological responses, our body is instantaneously preparing for fight or flight. Automatic biological and psychological processes are putting us in a state of readiness either to defend against or to escape the perceived danger. The emotional content within this arousal pattern includes the twin feelings of anger and fear.

Have you awakened in the night to a sound that makes you think someone has broken into your home or apartment? Or has someone cut you off on the expressway? Remember how instantaneously your body shifted into readiness—heart beating wildly, palms sweating, stomach and jaw muscles tense. Remember the mixed emotions—fear that you could be hurt and anger that someone dared to invade your private space or run you off the road. In summary, when you feel angry, either you or something or somebody important to you is being threatened.

The intensity of our anger in response to a particular threat is related to our perception of the size of the danger—the higher our level of threat, the stronger our emotional response. If the threat is minor we feel mild irritation or frustration and hardly notice the arousal pattern. If the threat is major, however, our emotional response will be intense. Because you have much at stake in your marriage, this relationship probably generates more threat than most. Our sense of self is more vulnerable in this relationship and we have higher expectations.

The potential for anger is universal. All persons in all cultures experience anger because to be human is to be faced with various physical, social, and psychological threats. Depending on culture and personality, each person experiences threat in a unique manner and expresses anger according to cultural norms. Notice that in the same situation one person will feel threatened while another will not. Why? Because our selves are invested in different values and beliefs so that a particular action may be perceived as a threat by one spouse but not by the other.

Because of values about togetherness and some fear about being alone, I (Judy) began our marriage with the belief that if husbands loved their wives they would not travel except in emergency situations. When Andy chose to travel for professional meetings and speaking engagements, I was threatened and angry about his choice. Though some friends could identify with my feelings, I knew other men and women with different belief systems who were not threatened in the least when their spouse chose to travel.

WHAT DOES THE BIBLE SAY?

Given the universal character of the human capacity for experiencing anger in the face of a threat to self, we must conclude that this capacity is part of the created order. Some Christians respond as if anger was a result of evil and should be avoided by those who want to live according to God's purposes. This capacity for anger, however, is rooted in God's creation, not sin. It has been part of being human from the beginning and is necessary for our survival. The natural reaction of being anxious, angry, and fearful of that which we perceive to be threatening is part of the reality of being human that was blessed by God in Genesis 1:31 as being "very good."

If you have been taught that to be angry is sinful, you may assume that scripture supports the idea that "good" Christians don't *show* anger and the "best" Christians don't even *feel* angry. Actually, the Bible takes for granted that the experience of anger is part of the human condition. Jesus, for example, was angry on numerous occasions, but perhaps the best known is when he entered the temple: "Making a whip of cords, he drove all of them out of the temple, both the sheep and the cattle. He also poured out the coins of the money changers and overturned their tables" (John 2:15). On the cross, Jesus felt abandoned by God and spoke words of anger about being deserted: "My God, my God, why have you forsaken me?" (Mark 15:34). And in the gospel of Mark, in response to the legalism of the religious leaders who were blind to their own lack of compassion, Jesus "looked around at them with anger" (3:5). If Jesus is a model for living the Christian life, then his example makes apparent that being angry is not necessarily contradictory to the way of love.

The Bible tells many stories about God getting angry. Since we are created in the image of God, it follows that we would have this same potential for anger. The Bible is also clear that anger can lead to sin and warns us that when we are angry we are more likely to be destructive. The writer of Ephesians, for example, begins a commentary on anger with the phrase, "Be angry but do not sin" (4:26). Notice the assumption conveyed by this statement is that everyone gets angry. The author is concerned that we guard against sinning with our anger, for when we are angry we are more vulnerable to sin. In summary, the *experience* of anger is not sinful, but *expressions* of anger can certainly be sinful.

An early example comes from the Cain and Abel story found in Genesis 4:3–7. Cain's sin is often thought to be his anger, but the story plainly shows otherwise. The Lord was obviously concerned that Cain "was very angry" and even asked him, "Why are you angry?" Rather than accusing Cain of sinning by being angry, the Lord warns Cain of his vulnerability to sin: "Sin is lurking at the door; its desire is for you, but you must master it." Our point is that the experience of anger was not deemed a sin by the Lord, but Cain did have responsibility for handling his anger creatively rather than destructively. So it is with marriage partners—when we are angry we are more vulnerable to sin against one another. As Cain chose to destroy his brother Abel, we will hurt each other and destroy our marriage unless we accept responsibility for handling anger creatively.

You can see from the Bible's point of view that the potential for anger is rooted in God's created order rather than in our sinful nature. The capacity for anger in the face of threat has been with us since the beginning, not after sin came into the world. In fact the capacity for anger is a gift from God which serves the dual purpose of making us aware of when we are in danger and providing the physiological readiness and the psychological motivation to survive through fight or flight.

Within your marriage anger can be perceived as a warning signal that enables you to identify and react against destructive forces which threaten the relationship. When anger is viewed in this positive light, it can be claimed, acknowledged, and celebrated. Anger can both give life and destroy life, energize relationships and destroy relationships. We are the ones responsible for how we use this capacity.

FACING ANGER AND CONFLICT
WITH INTEGRITY

Many couples participate in marriage enrichment events and enter marriage counseling asking the basic question, "How can we deal more

IT TAKES TWO

creatively with our anger and conflict?" For people of faith the answer must include an ethical perspective. Why? Because we don't have much control over the *experience* of anger (the arousal symptoms), but we do have control over how we act in this aroused state. We can choose to behave in ways that erode love and are destructive to the relationship (becoming enraged, cold, hostile, withdrawn, abusive) or we can respond in ways that lead to new levels of intimacy.

As people who believe the good news that Jesus is our peace and has broken down the dividing walls of hostility as described in Ephesians 2:14, we are committed to peacemaking. We are called to the "ministry of reconciliation" (2 Cor. 5:18) so we have responsibility to respond to anger and conflict in a way that leads toward bridging the estrangement. We are committed from a faith perspective, therefore, to handle our anger in creative ways that express our love and deepen intimacy. Below we describe some basic principles for handling anger with integrity and within the context of Christian ethics.

Creating a Safe Place

One barrier to confronting anger openly and creatively is the fear generated by both our anger and the anger of our partner: fear of judgment, rejection, abandonment, losing the relationship, and even physical harm. What are we to do in the face of this fear? Remembering what love does to fear would be a good start.

> There is no fear in love, but perfect love casts out fear; for fear has to
> do with punishment, and whoever fears has not reached perfection
> in love. (1 John 4:18)

This wise observation teaches us that growing toward "perfection in love" means deciding to remove fear from conflict. As we strive for maturity in our love we must set ground rules which enable basic trust to be the context for handling conflict and anger. We must be intentional to avoid any action which generates fear in our partner. The two major ways of creating fear are physical intimidation (grabbing, shaking, slapping, pushing, or more extensive violence) and verbal threats about harmful consequences (divorce, abandonment).

How can we remove our partner's fear that our anger will hurt or destroy? We can make a commitment not to do harm. Pledging not to get angry would be unrealistic and foolhardy, but we can make a covenant not to hurt the other when we are angry (see chapter 8 on making covenants). Since we can control what we *do* with our anger, such a covenant establishes a context of security, a safety zone that allows a more creative response to anger. Such a commitment to love and justice enables us to deal with anger openly and honestly because we trust that whatever occurs, neither partner will be rejected, abandoned, or damaged by physical or emotional abuse. After all, the scripture does not say "perfect love casts out *anger*" but that "perfect love casts out *fear*."

BLESSED is the one whose spouse can be trusted *not* to abuse.

Developing an Early Warning System

To be responsible with our anger we must know when it occurs. Many of us are only aware of our anger after we have lashed out, or resentfully withdrawn. The earlier we become aware that we are becoming angry the better our chance to "master it" (as the Lord challenged Cain to do), to call on our rational and spiritual resources for dealing with it constructively. Being ethical with anger includes increasing our awareness of when we are feeling angry. This awareness allows us to be clear with both our self and our spouse about our anger before it reaches destructive proportions. Temper tantrums, for example, are unnecessary if a spouse identifies the early signs and chooses other options.

You may be thinking, "Well anger just suddenly appears; how can I possibly know in advance?" If you are a person whose anger comes to the surface quickly, you need to sharpen your awareness of the physical arousal patterns so that you gain a few minutes of awareness that anger is on the way. You can then take control of it rather than allowing it to control you. If you are a person whose anger seems to come slowly, remember that anger does not occur without leaving telltale signs—physical, emotional, and behavioral clues. You can develop your own early warning system by learning your unique symptoms.

EXERCISE: Identifying Symptoms of Anger

Play detective and discover the unique clues that allow you to know quickly that you are angry. Invite your spouse to help you with this exercise.

1. Start with the physical. How does your body announce that you are angry? Common signals include muscular tension (clenched teeth, tightness in the stomach, pursed lips, flared nostrils), cardiovascular irregularities (accelerated heartbeat, flushed face, sweating, headaches, angina), and gastrointestinal upset (gas, heartburn, indigestion, diarrhea).

2. What about emotional clues—your moods? When you are cranky, frustrated, disappointed, sullen, irritated, touchy, and so forth, then you are probably experiencing some level of anger.

3. Identify patterns of behavior that occur when you are angry: speaking sarcastically, withdrawing, slamming the door, withholding affection, going to the refrigerator for food you don't need, and so forth. Other signs of anger include relating to your spouse in a manner that is demanding, discounting, shaming, labeling, blaming, withholding, controlling, or ridiculing. You can assume that any behaviors which hurt, demean, or sabotage your spouse grow out of anger.

Keeping Anger Out in the Open

Fleeing from conflict and refusing to confront are common ways of responding to our fear and trembling in the face of anger. Avoidance is problematic, however, because anger that is ignored or swallowed will often surface in destructive ways. The admonition in Ephesians, "Do not let the sun go down on your anger, and do not make room for the devil" (4:26–27), reveals the author's awareness that suppressing anger makes us vulnerable to its demonic power. When we hide our anger in the back pockets of our mind and heart it becomes destructive. Why? Because we lose the capacity to use our rational, volitional, and spiritual resources to direct the anger in creative, loving directions. We also lose the opportunity to use the "anger event" as a "diagnostic window" through which to learn something new about ourselves and our relationship.

In most cases, angry feelings that are not identified, expressed, and resolved, make us more vulnerable to intensified arousal at the next experience of anger.

> Joy grew up with an immature mother who had a series of marriages and other relationships. As the oldest child, Joy often took over the role of homemaker and mother to younger siblings while she was an adolescent. This became a pattern of relating that Joy carried throughout her young adulthood without ever dealing with the chronic anger she felt about the burdens which unfairly fell on her shoulders. If she expressed any negative feelings her mother responded irrationally, so to maintain peace Joy became an expert at "stuffing" the angry feelings.
>
> When she married she continued this pattern. When she got angry at her husband, Wayne, she suppressed it. She would go for awhile without saying anything about what was bothering her and then suddenly she would "have a fit" around some event which did not deserve such intensity. Wayne's response was to withdraw and he began staying away more frequently. When they came to therapy they had to deal with her tendency to store anger. She had to learn to identify when she was angry, communicate this with Wayne, and clearly state what she needed. This gave him the opportunity to respond more creatively.

Anger which goes unattended is put in a psychic "storehouse" and over time, like food left in the open, it "goes bad." It becomes bitterness, jealousy, hostility, and hatred which leads to destructive words and actions. These destructive expressions of anger are what Jesus is speaking against in the Sermon on the Mount.

> You have heard that it was said to those of ancient times, "You shall not murder"; and "whoever murders shall be liable to judgment." But I say to you that if you are angry with a brother or sister, you will be liable to judgment . . . (Matt. 5:21–22)

These verses have been quoted to suggest that feeling angry is the same as committing murder. The Greek verb translated "are angry," however, is a present participle and refers to continuous action. More accurate translations are those by Charles Williams: "everyone who harbors malice against," and the New English Bible, "anyone who nurses anger against," which clearly show that Jesus is not talking about every experience of anger. Rather, he is addressing those who allow unresolved anger to fester in their hearts until it breaks forth in destructive behavior. Later in verse 22, Jesus gives examples of this destructive behavior—insulting others and calling them fools.

Keeping up-to-date with anger is important so that we don't permit one particular experience of anger to infect another. Anger piled upon anger raises the level of tension until the anger gets out of control. When couples keep up-to-date with their anger they can reduce the amount of voltage triggered by the same event at another time. A practical commitment can be to "name it, claim it, reframe it, and tame it" so that an experience of anger does not bury itself in the back of our minds and hearts where it can influence later behavior. That way the partners will learn something from the anger event, since any experience of anger can be the proverbial "tip of the iceberg" of a deeper threat that needs to be uncovered and resolved.

Al and Stella argued constantly about how to spend money, but the deeper threat to Al was his need for economic security and his fear that their spending patterns would jeopardize their future.

Kerry got frustrated frequently with Hazel's pattern of staying up late, saying that it was hard for him to get to sleep without her. His real concern was that she did not want to spend time with him in sexual encounters.

Often an occurrence of anger comes minutes before company is coming, or when one partner needs to leave for work or is on the way to an engagement, so that fully dealing with the event is not possible. The danger is that this event will be "forgotten" because the partners either forget, or do not want to revisit this uncomfortable emotion and cause conflict. A more effective choice is for the partner to name the angry feelings and request that the situation be put on the couple's agenda for some later conversation.

Being Honest

The writer of Ephesians says, "But speaking the truth in love, we must grow up . . . into Christ" (4:15). Partners must be willing to tell the truth as a central commitment to maintaining love. There is a crucial connection between caring for another and confronting. We can measure the depth of our love by the amount of honest confrontation which is expressed in a relationship. Jesus cared enough to confront; can we love any less honestly?

Pretending we are not angry by masking it with a smile, or speaking words that contradict our deeper feelings, is dishonest. Deceiving our spouse is a lie (to use a harsh word) and threatens the trust so basic to intimacy. We deceive by misrepresenting data ("The door slammed accidentally"), giving false interpretations ("I didn't know that would upset you"), and masking feelings (forcing a smile instead of frowning). In short, the sacred revelatory process of communication discussed in chapter 3 is distorted and our spouse is tricked into responding to a false reality.

When expressing concern about "not sinning with our anger," the author of Ephesians writes, "So then, putting away falsehood, let all of us speak the truth to our neighbors" (4:25). Assuming that our spouse counts as a neighbor (for sure!) we have an ethical responsibility to deal honestly with our emotional life, including anger. A spouse has the right to know what is on our minds and hearts, particularly the emotional content. Attempting to hide anger reveals a breakdown in one's integrity.

Accepting Responsibility

Taking responsibility for our anger includes admitting that our partner, though triggering the angry event, didn't make us angry. We got angry because something our partner did or said (or didn't do or say) threatened us. To handle anger with integrity means acknowledging that anger starts out as our problem; after all, we are the ones who are threatened.

After claiming responsibility for your angry response, you can move toward the decision about whether being threatened in this situation is appropriate or necessary. Is your partner part of the problem by her or his words and actions? Have you been treated unjustly? Have you been discounted, ridiculed, rejected, manipulated? Or is your interpretation of your spouse's words and actions as a threat basically your problem? That is, you must examine the situation to see if it is your immaturity, sensitivity, unmet needs, and so forth that set you up to feel threatened.

> BLESSED is the couple in which each partner
> accepts responsibility for her or his own anger.

CREATIVE CONFRONTING

Jesus' words in the Sermon on the Mount, "Blessed are the peacemakers, for they will be called children of God" (Matt. 5:9), challenge both partners to be responsible for taking initiatives toward peace and reconciliation. Christian love feels protective of community and does so by being proactive rather than passive when anger threatens to disrupt the peace. There are certainly situations in marriage when one partner waits patiently on the other, but the occasion of anger is not normally one of them. The sooner anger is out in the open, the more likely we can minimize the harm and move toward reconciliation. To act quickly and creatively (whether we are the angry partner or perceiving anger in our spouse) is to trust the Spirit to guide us back toward resolution and intimacy. Deciding to be honest and proactive raises the next question: How can you creatively communicate to your spouse that you are angry?

Initiating Conversation about Your Anger

Take a deep breath and plunge ahead. Start by communicating in your own words and style, "I need to share with you that I am experiencing anger." When anger is identified or described (instead of "spit out" or "thrown"), your spouse does not have to feel accused or attacked. Besides, with a "commitment not to harm" covenant in place, your partner will not have to be afraid. If you think he or she will become defensive and react before hearing you through, find a way to ask for a full hearing—"I might have trouble expressing myself; will you let me talk for ten minutes before you say anything?"

After getting your partner's attention, and agreeing on your need to speak without interruption for a few minutes, you can elaborate on the situation. Describe what you experienced, how you perceive the situation, what you are feeling, and what you need (use the awareness wheel discussed in chapter 3). "I am angry because . . ." or "I became angry when . . ." become initial forays into the dialogue. You won't know everything about your experience of anger, but you can communicate what you know at that moment.

> BLESSED is the one whose spouse
> puts feelings of anger on the table.

If anger has occurred between the two of you (angry words expressed or actions taken) but no resolution took place, you can be the one to initiate conversation at a later time. "I would like to describe my feelings about the event yesterday and tell you what I know about what caused my anger. Would you listen to me for a few minutes?"

Involving Your Partner

Though you are the angry partner, and accept primary responsibility for understanding your anger and resolving your feelings, remember that your anger is a threat to the relationship. Therefore, after communicating your anger, invite your spouse to join you in examining other possible sources of threat. Demonstrate that you are taking responsibility for your anger but want to invite her or him to join you in discovering the causes (threats) and working out a resolution that will contribute to intimacy. After all, your spouse also has an investment in moving through the anger toward resolution and, if some harm has been done, forgiveness and reconciliation (see chapter 7).

Your spouse knows you better than almost anyone else and can offer invaluable assistance in uncovering the multiple levels of threat that ignited anger. Naturally, identifying potential solutions will probably involve your spouse, because he or she will have to concur with changes that can reduce the threats.

Entering a Covenant

Now that the anger is on the table and the threats identified, you can choose to change behavior and move toward resolution and reconciliation. Translate what you have learned into a need and work on a covenant as described in chapter 8.

EXERCISE: Covenant Making to Reduce a Frustration

A process for changing behavior called covenant making is introduced in the last section of chapter 8. Choose a current frustration and identify the threat. Then follow the covenant-making procedures and make a behavior change that reduces the threat.

Note: If you cannot reach an understanding of your anger, or continue to sabotage your covenants, give yourself the gift of several sessions with a professional counselor. Commit to discovering and resolving the deeper issues sparking the anger so that the alienation can be bridged. When anger and conflict are becoming painful, seeking a third party to help the process becomes the responsible next step. If anger is already intense, consider seeing a counselor now, before it becomes more destructive.

WHAT CAN YOU DO
WHEN YOUR PARTNER IS ANGRY?

Both partners have responsibility for increasing self-awareness by learning to identify anger when it occurs in the relationship. We pick up both verbal and nonverbal signals from our partners about their emotional state of mind and heart. You may realize that your spouse is angry even though he or she is not communicating such awareness. When your partner is angry, you are tempted to make several responses depending on your personality and your family story.

Being Defensive

You can feel offended that your partner would dare to be angry at you, assuming immediately that the anger is undeserved (which may be true), and move into a defensive posture. Then you will rationalize, stonewall, and otherwise resist your spouse's anger. In numerous verbal and nonverbal ways you will claim that the problem is hers or his, leading to further conflict.

Feeling Guilty

You can assume that something is wrong with you and feel guilty. If you have low self-esteem, or were raised in a shame-based family, you will automatically assume you are at fault and accept blame for the spouse's anger. This posture confirms an over/under relationship, with you in the under position, and makes you, the supposed guilty partner, vulnerable to injustice.

Counterattacking

When your spouse has expressed anger in hurtful ways, your first impulse may be to punish her or him for the transgression. You choose to counterattack ("I'll teach you to get angry with me!"). When we counterattack our motivation shifts from wanting to love to trying to win. We want to force the partner to give up. We would like to prove her wrong or make him feel guilty. The desire for intimacy is taken over by the desire for victory, fighting in ways that we think will cause the other to surrender and admit defeat. Reversing this process is not easy, but interrupting the win/lose cycle of yelling and screaming, or silence and withdrawal, is important. Words and actions which hurt are difficult to overcome.

Listening and Responding Creatively

Ideally, however, when we suspect that our partner is angry we will take responsibility to approach him or her about our perceptions. How can we avoid being defensive, feeling guilty, or counterattacking and instead initiate a creative response? It is helpful to remember that your partner is angry because he or she has been threatened by some word or deed. Communicate with your spouse that you want to form an alliance to find out what has gone wrong.

Be more creative than to ask the proverbial "What's wrong?" question. The answer will usually be either a noncommittal "Nothing" or a further outburst, "You should know!" A better choice is to use the communication skills from chapter three to express your perceptions of what

IT TAKES TWO

is happening and your desire to participate in a process of figuring out what can be changed to creatively dissolve the anger. You can volunteer to participate in naming the threat so that something can be resolved.

> BLESSED is the one whose spouse tries to be
> first to initiate a cease-fire.

If your partner's anger has been expressed inappropriately, you feel hurt or rejected. Then what? According to Jesus in Matthew 18:15–17, the person who feels wronged or treated unjustly should initiate the reconciliation process: "If another member of the church sins against you, go and point out the fault when the two of you are alone" (18:15; also see Matt. 5:23–24). This is accomplished when the victimized partner takes responsibility for communicating the feelings of hurt, sadness, and rejection being experienced in the face of the spouse's anger. Use the awareness wheel to describe your response as thoroughly as possible.

HOW ARE HUSBANDS
AND WIVES DIFFERENT?

The first truth to identify about gender differences around anger is that men and women have equal amounts of it. A common misperception is to think that men experience more anger than women. However, research shows that in similar circumstances women and men rate their level of anger the same. But there is a reason for the misperception; men and women are socialized, generally speaking, to experience and express anger differently.

Female Socialization

Women often are socialized to be patient and kind regardless of the provocation. When taught this response, women are supposed to "take it," and an angry response of any kind is perceived to be unfeminine. When women speak angrily they may be described as "bitchy," accused of having no sense of humor, identified as "too sensitive," or labeled a hot-headed feminist.

Women often associate anger and aggression with selfishness and chaos. If they have been the central linchpin in family stability, the one responsible for domestic tranquillity, they may find it difficult to allow themselves to experience anger or act aggressively. Their concern is that such feelings and actions would disrupt the family, making them feel irresponsible. Women often find tension between their commitments to peace and harmony on the one hand and their need to express anger on the other. They may suppress anger as long as possible. Then when they do express it, they may feel that they are in the wrong. Instead of feeling relieved at having expressed themselves they may be filled with shame and guilt.

Wives who have been raised in this manner have to be alert to the effect of this socialization process in the marital relationship. You can resist letting your anger build up under the guise of keeping everything calm and collected. You are not the person responsible for maintaining the peace at any price. Such suppression leads to physical and emotional stress, depression, unnecessary explosions, or nondirect methods of expressing anger that compromise intimacy (silence, complaining to other friends, dumping it on the children, withdrawing sexually, spending money unwisely). Many women in therapy and in enrichment events describe the seething fury they feel about certain aspects of the marriage, usually feeling powerless to do anything to change the status quo. Your willingness to take a more direct approach, as described earlier, can make a difference. By all means, if you do express anger don't let guilt or shame make you apologize too quickly and suppress the feelings.

Male Socialization

Men are socialized, generally speaking, to think of anger more positively as a necessary part of life and aggression as an appropriate response. Most males are given permission to be direct with anger, to express verbally or act out physically with their anger. Men are often applauded for aggression, given higher status for being tough and fighting back. They may learn that aggressive response with anger is the "manly" thing to do.

> Andy was told by his father to do what he could to avoid a fight, but if he had to defend his honor, his father instructed him to "pick up the biggest stick you can find and make sure you win." We doubt that any of his sisters were given the same advice.

To be perceived as a sissy or to appear wimpy is to risk losing esteem in the eyes of peers and male mentors (fathers, coaches, sergeants, and bosses, for example). A male often needs to express anger aggressively, whether verbally (trash talking, threats, boasting) or physically (fighting, playing sports with the intention to hurt), in order to maintain self-esteem.

Men are often taught to use aggression instrumentally, as a way of gaining power over another. When men are unable to have their way by reasoning, or by charm, they may choose aggressive expressions of anger in order to have their way. Men have been known to force obedience, particularly with wives and children, in order to enhance or recover self-esteem.

Husbands who have been brought up this way must beware of the temptation to express anger with the intent of intimidation and gaining the power over position. Such intensity causes fear and alienation, which is hard to repair. Men, you may have to guard against becoming physical in ways that literally hurt your wife. Remember that even if you are consciously committed to an egalitarian relationship, you may have been socialized to have the traditional position of being the head of the family. Beneath your awareness may be the feeling that you have the right to be in charge of your wife and children.

Fear

Men and women are often afraid of their anger for different reasons. Women are more likely to be afraid that dealing straightforwardly with anger will break the relationship, that the man will leave. If she was brought up by parents who withdrew love and approval, or physically separated when they were angry, she will be even more vulnerable to this threat, fearing that anger could cause the dissolution of the marriage.

Russell came from a traditional family and community in west Texas ranch country. He firmly believed that he was the "lord of his castle" and that all decisions and opinions expressed in the home were to be his. His wife, Patricia, began the marriage with the same assumptions, but over time came to believe that she too deserved a voice in decisions, particularly about issues that affected her. Being cut off by Russell when she spoke and having her opinions dismissed, Patricia began to voice her anger when her growing sense of self became threatened. She grew to understand that God had created her with intelligence and the right to express opinions. She began verbalizing different ideas than those expressed by Russell and giving input to the decision-making process. His sense of masculine esteem became threatened. His first response was to become quiet. After several of these events, however, he became verbally aggressive.

Men are afraid first of all that their anger will be ineffective. Losing the conflict could cause a loss of status and self-esteem. If their first expressions of anger don't seem to be effective with someone they feel they should control, like a wife, then they may escalate their expressions of anger as a way of overpowering the opponent and gaining acquiescence.

When Russell became threatened by Patricia's actions he became intimidating with his anger. He attacked her for being a poor wife, for undercutting his role, and thinking "she was better than me." He became verbally abusive by calling her names.

When anger gets this intense, males often fear that they will lose control and go into a rage that will be either emotionally or physically harmful.

Russell withdrew from the house several times for fear that he would "become physical" with Patricia. When she suggested counseling, he agreed (though reluctantly) largely because of his fear that he would become physically abusive and that such behavior would end the marriage.

Females often fear this same possibility, knowing that the physical difference in size and strength makes them vulnerable to physical force. In fact, many women have personally experienced physical violence from males or have witnessed it through family and friends. Females can also express anger violently, of course, but this capability rarely creates fear in males. Beyond the physical fear is the anxiety over the possibility of abandonment.

Patricia became frightened when the anger escalated into verbal abuse. Though "he has never touched me," she had a deep fear that in an uncontrollable moment "the unthinkable" could happen. She suppressed her own anger for a while, primarily because of her fear that he would leave. At this point she suggested marriage counseling.

Crying

Many women express frustration at their tendency to cry when angry, because crying often blunts their ability to finish expressing the anger in clear fashion. Having swallowed her anger over a period of time, a woman may have built up significant tension. When she finally attempts to express the anger, tears may come as the less threatening discharge of this tension. As one woman expressed,

> For me anger is so closely bound up with crying. I can't remember getting angry and not crying first of all. I think it's bound up with being kind of helpless. I have guilty feelings about actually being angry to begin with . . . I usually break down in tears. I feel so overpowered by the anger, and I really don't know how to express it. I feel like I really don't know how to be appropriately angry . . . so I get very frustrated and then I cry (see p. 46 in the book by Campbell listed in "For Further Reading" at the end of this chapter).

Husbands can resist the temptation to interpret these kinds of tears as weakness or remorse. Hear it as an expression of anger that needs to be taken as seriously as you would take an expression of anger from a male. Don't laugh and tell her she is cute when she's angry. She isn't cute; she is mad, and that isn't funny. Don't try to comfort these kind of tears; that will only make her more angry because of your insensitivity to her deep rage. You might find yourself afraid and threatened by the tears because you feel guilty, but resist the temptation to interpret the crying as manipulative. Instead, *listen!* Invite her to tell you what is happening inside her.

Wives can resist allowing the embarrassment over crying to keep them from finding direct ways to express anger. If you do cry, there is no need to apologize. Ask your husband to wait until you are through and can resume, or talk right through the tears.

Talking It Through

Another problem comes in the different ways males and females may be socialized to deal with anger. A woman usually has learned to talk it through until some resolution is reached. As we described in the communication chapter, she has learned to use conversation as a way of establishing and maintaining relationships and certainly as the major vehicle for conflict resolution. Males use conversation more for dealing with information and establishing hierarchy and control in relationships. When the wife becomes angry, the husband is more likely to discuss facts without attending to the more complex emotional intensity of his wife. He may even refuse to talk about the "problem" because he doesn't feel there is one, or is threatened by it. This frustrates her even more and increases the anger because of his unwillingness to talk and be "emotionally available." Men must work overtime at taking the risk to identify their deeper feelings and be able to engage their wives in meaningful conversation about those things which make her angry.

As a husband it is important to realize that when your wife is angry, her desire is not to challenge you. Unlike the males in your world, she doesn't want to have a contest to see who wins. What she wants is to be taken seriously, to have her feelings and experiences acknowledged, to know that you are concerned with what bothers her, and that the relationship is important to you. She does not want her anger to push you away, but on the contrary, desires to be connected with you. You will be tempted to respond as if your control or status is being challenged, or as if you are being accused. Resist the internal call to fight. Instead, let her know that you recognize that since she is angry there must be something between the two of you that needs attention and that you are committed to finding out what is wrong. Sit back and hear her out. The resulting intimacy is the gift she wants and will be meaningful to you as well.

As a wife look for intentional ways to express yourself if your emotional responses are threatening to your husband. Use the awareness wheel from chapter 3 and ask him to let you describe your reactions for ten minutes before he speaks. Perhaps a letter could describe your responses to the event in a way he could hear.

WHY *ARE* YOU ANGRY?
UNDERSTANDING THE THREAT

After the anger is identified and both partners committed to resolution, the next step is to seek out the source of the threat. After noticing

Cain's anger, God asked, "Why are you angry?" (Gen. 4:6). This is still the basic question with which the angry person (and hopefully the partner) must grapple. What happened? Why did I get angry? This is using the anger event as a "diagnostic window" through which to gain self-understanding about why you are angry. The answers potentially lead toward deeper levels of self-awareness, from which the process of growth and reconciliation begin.

Each spouse has walked a different road, at different speeds, and in different shoes. Personality differences, for example, can be threatening to both partners. If one partner is quick to act in any situation (the car won't start again, so she wants to go buy another one today) and the other needs time to consider all the alternatives (perhaps we should find out what is wrong and evaluate our finances), then the behavior of either is likely to be experienced by the other as a threat.

As we pointed out in chapter 2, our individual stories are different. Like a ship's log or the black box of an airliner, they reveal a unique journey. The difference in our stories (family history, experience, knowledge) can make a meaningful contribution to the richness of the marriage, but they are also a source of conflict (see chapter 2). Each spouse's story contains a certain worldview that includes values, lifestyles, and psychosocial needs (see chapter 4). We tend to invest our worldview, our values, and our lifestyles with a sense of rightness. That is, we identify them with what is "best," "good," even "Christian," and assume that someone who takes an opposite approach is somehow "wrong," "sinful," "dumb," or "unchristian," rather than different. Here are some specific sources of threat for you to consider.

Clashing Values

Each partner brings into the marriage beliefs and philosophies about every aspect of life, from parenting to patterns of spending money.

Paul and Chris describe a constant source of anger and conflict in their different concepts of time. They constantly argue over when to leave for church and social engagements. Chris believes that being on time means "being five minutes early." Paul believes he is on time if he is "only fifteen minutes late." Over a few sessions they began to examine the threats to each of them. Chris believes that "responsible" people are on time in any situation. Therefore, when Paul "makes them late" she is threatened because she feels irresponsible, she is embarrassed to be married to someone who is irresponsible, and she feels unloved by Paul because he does not care enough about her to be on time. Paul, on the other hand, gets threatened if he functions with her definition of being on time because he wastes time since "nothing ever happens for the first fifteen minutes," feels embarrassed by Chris' "compulsiveness," feels attacked by her accusations that he is irresponsible, and does not like the feeling of being ordered around.

They worked on a covenant that included three new ideas. First, given Paul's responsible approach to life in other areas, Chris would recognize that given his worldview about time, he was not being irresponsible and she would resist accusing him of this character flaw. Next, given her strong need to be on time by her definition, they would discuss each engagement and decide in advance whether it was a situation in which she felt the need to arrive on time. If it was, he would go on her time frame and take something to read. Finally, if they disagreed they would try for a month to take separate cars.

For the most part, Paul decided that since this was so important for Chris, and mattered little to him, that he would realize he was not being ordered around and show his love by being on time by her definition. On the other hand, she accepted that there were situations when being there "on the dot" didn't really matter. They significantly reduced the amount of anger that had previously been experienced.

Conflicting Lifestyles

Each partner comes from a different family with a different lifestyle about everything, from how to take a vacation to table manners. When our spouse functions with a lifestyle different than the one we have learned to value, it may threaten our sense of etiquette, appropriate behavior, or our ideas about what good people "should" do.

Teresa and Ishmael, married for two years, described a major cause of anger and conflict in a marriage enrichment seminar. Ishmael's father worked for a tire manufacturing plant that always closed down for two weeks in August. During those two weeks his family, who were not high on the economic ladder, prided themselves in saving money by vacationing at home. Furthermore, they saved money by choosing to complete a task that "would have cost a bundle if someone else had done it," such as painting the house or fixing the roof. Ishmael remembers one summer when the family received an estimate of $2,000 to paint the house, then did the job themselves and enjoyed saving the money.

Teresa's family, on the other hand, always used vacation time to take a trip away from home, having anticipated over many months the new things they would see. They opened a special account at the bank after each vacation in order to save money for the next year's trip. Their vacations were the highlight of their year and the time when the family felt most together. Many of her family stories revolved around these special vacations.

What did this couple discover about the threats? As Ishmael said, if he and Teresa spent $2,000 on a vacation he was "down $4,000—the $2,000 we spent and the $2,000 we didn't save!" He was threatened by the financial setback for something he had not learned to value as "a way of doing life." She was used to a lifestyle that included vacations as a major way of family bonding. If they did not go on a trip, Teresa felt cheated and unloved by a husband who would not join her in the exciting process of planning for and saving toward a vacation.

They made a covenant that satisfied them both. Ishmael would meet Teresa's need to plan and enjoy vacations by agreeing to go on trips during their vacation time. They agreed to do as much maintenance on their house as they could, but on weekends rather than during vacation. To meet Ishmael's needs not to spend too much money, Teresa agreed that for the next three years they would take vacations within driving distance.

Unmet Needs and Expectations

When we marry we expect that our spouse's love for us will lead her or him to respond to our wants and desires in whatever way will make us happy (see chapter 8). We assume that meeting our needs will be one of her or his prime goals. When this does not happen, or when our partner does not seem to care about a particular need, we feel threatened.

When Gary refused to go to her cousin's wedding in a town three hours south of their home, Cheryl got so angry that they came to see a counselor. She is constantly angry at his disinterest and unwillingness to participate in activities away from the house or be with people unless he is at work.

Gary is a shy introvert who feels threatened in social situations by the possibility that he "won't know what to say," "might say something wrong," or "feel stupid." Cheryl, on the other hand, is gregarious. She enjoys social settings and conversation with others. She needs and thrives on having many relationships and social encounters. When Gary continuously finds excuses not to attend any group functions, she feels threatened in several ways. First, she values family togetherness, but she either has to stay home or go by herself, which makes her feel like "half a family." Next, she feels treated unfairly because marriage is a "two-way street" and if "I am willing to stay home sometimes he should be willing to go with me at other times." Last, she feels unloved because he doesn't overcome his fear in order to meet one of her important needs.

We not only expect our spouse to meet our needs, but we have expectations about *how* he or she will do it. The wedding openly addresses some of our commitments in the vows, but at unrecognized levels we assume our spouse is entering into a contract that spells out the way we will live together. This contract is informed by each partner's stories about marriage. These stories are informed by the family in which we grew up, the media, the larger societal context, and our individual fantasies. When this unspoken, perhaps unrecognized, agreement is broken by the spouse, our ideal for the marriage is threatened. If the expectation is strong, the seeming breach of contract may feel like betrayal.

Shonda and Clayton have been married four years and have a two-year-old daughter. Clayton is director of an inner city social ministry sponsored by several churches. When he married he assumed that Shonda, who was knowledgeable and committed to his work, would be supportive. Clayton was threatened by "her disinterest in my ministry." As Clayton was able to state in a counseling session, he thinks for her to be supportive means attending most of the functions, giving time and energy to the work, listening to him talk about the problems, and understanding that his job would demand much of his time at night and leave him frequently preoccupied with his work.

Shonda felt supportive of Clayton, but she assumed that marriage would bring family into the forefront of his mind. She assumed that they would have dinner together most nights, share about life, share parenting of their daughter, and spend time being together in the evenings. She was threatened by her husband's "being married to the work and not to me." They both assumed that needs for support and togetherness would be met in certain ways and were threatened when the partner did not respond as expected.

One way of addressing the source of threat is to change "I am angry!" statements and feelings into an "I need———" statement. Such a transformed sentence may reveal the source of threat and allow a beginning point for resolving the anger.

Clayton was able to decide which of his needs was strongest and then state, "I need you to spend time listening to me talk about my work." Shonda was able to state her primary need as, "I need to feel like a family around meals and parenting." They worked hard to develop a covenant which would meet both needs. The final shape of their covenant included reserving one half hour on three days a week during which they would only talk about his work, spending two nights a week and twice on the weekend eating dinner together at the table without TV, and having Clayton read to their daughter and put her to bed two nights a week.

Being Treated Unfairly

We will discuss the importance of justice in a Christian marriage in chapter 7. For now we want to point out that if either spouse perceives that the relationship has become unfair, or that the partner has behaved unjustly, then he or she will experience this development as a threat.

Christine is angry at Sam because, although they both hold down full-time employment, he plays golf all weekend and leaves most child care and family maintenance to her. She feels that this division of labor is unfair and that she is treated unjustly. She has difficulty maintaining any sense of intimacy because of the anger.

Maxwell and Andrea fight over an issue that leaves him feeling as if an injustice has occurred. She feels obligated to spend Saturday evenings and Sunday mornings with her widowed father at his home eighty-six miles away. She says her father needs her, but Maxwell notices that the father doesn't do anything on his own because he waits for Andrea to do it. He thinks her father has become dependent on Andrea. The fact that she spends each weekend away from him feels unfair.

EXERCISE: What Is the Threat?

In the following exercise you will find a list of unfinished sentences. Complete the sentences as honestly as possible. Couples use many words to describe anger, several of which you will find in this exercise, but please substitute your own vocabulary. When completed they will lead you to identify circumstances that create anger at your partner. If you think of other sentences that could help you identify "anger events" in your marriage, add them at the bottom.

After filling out the exercise, ask the question, "What are the threats behind these situations?" Use the concepts from above and from chapter 2 (clashing values, conflicting lifestyles, unmet needs, unfairness, and personality differences) as a way of assessing these conflicts.

Invite your spouse to help you think through the reasons why you are threatened in the situations you have described.

WHAT ABOUT PREVENTION?
REDUCING THREATS

One final ethical responsibility is to be intentional about prevention. It is our opportunity to identify those events, dynamics, and situations which do not have to threaten us. That is, those situations that, if we were more mature, would not have to threaten us and produce anger. Then we can choose attitudes and behaviors which reduce these threats and prevent the occurrence of anger.

Threat Identification Exercise

With your partner in mind, complete each of the following sentences:

We often argue over:

1._____

2._____

I get irritated when he or she:

1._____

2._____

I get frustrated when she or he:

1._____

2._____

I feel hurt when he or she:

1._____

2._____

We frequently disagree about:

1._____

2._____

I feel angry when she or he:

1._____

2._____

What are the possible threats behind these experiences?

Threat Identification Exercise

With your partner in mind, complete each of the following sentences:

We often argue over:

1._____

2._____

I get irritated when he or she:

1._____

2._____

I get frustrated when she or he:

1._____

2._____

I feel hurt when he or she:

1._____

2._____

We frequently disagree about:

1._____

2._____

I feel angry when she or he:

1._____

2._____

What are the possible threats behind these experiences?

- Understanding and identifying needs (see chapter 8) allows us to communicate to our partner what we need. Our partner can then help us meet those needs in satisfying ways. The threat that can be perceived when that need goes unmet is then reduced.
- Working as a couple to identify and clarify values and life-style choices that guide your life together can reduce the threats that occur when one of you acts on a value that is conflictual. As we discussed in chapter 2, the more you have created a couple story, the more you adopt shared values and lifestyles that guide choices and create a sense of partnership. Threats from clashing values and conflicting lifestyles are reduced.
- Likewise, understanding and naming personality differences allows couples to accept and even affirm the diverse manner in which they "do life." If behaviors that make these differences threatening can be identified, and covenants can be made that change those behaviors, then threats are lessened and anger reduced.
- Communication skills can be honed, as we described in chapter 3, so that you can avoid threats that arise from frustrations resulting from unclear communication.

This work to discern threats and work toward reducing them, and therefore the resultant anger, is the process of becoming "slow to anger," a spiritual development noted several times in Proverbs. Though the capacity to feel anger is one of God's gifts, we can certainly be destructive with this gift. It becomes our responsibility to note those things that threaten us so that we can reduce the amount of anger in our marriage and make sure that our relationship does not suffer from this "wear and tear" disease.

FOR FURTHER READING

Campbell, Anne. *Men, Women and Aggression*. New York: HarperCollins, Basic Books, 1993.

Lerner, Harriet Goldhor. *The Dance of Anger: A Woman's Guide to Changing the Patterns of Intimate Relationships*. New York: Harper & Row, 1985.

Lester, Andrew D. *Coping With Your Anger: A Christian Guide.* Philadelphia: Westminster Press, 1983.

Mace, David. *Love and Anger in Marriage.* Grand Rapids: Zondervan Publishing House, 1982.

Saussy, Carroll. *The Gift of Anger: A Call to Faithful Action.* Louisville, Ky.: Westminster John Knox Press, 1995.

Tavris, Carol. *Anger: The Misunderstood Emotion.* Revised Edition. New York: Simon & Schuster, 1989.

five

WHO'S THE BOSS?
Sharing Power and Responsibility

Does this chapter title surprise you? Are you wondering why we are discussing the issue of power? Hasn't the concept of equal rights prevailed, you ask, and the power issue settled? No. Many couples in our society are functioning, whether intentionally or not, in unequal relationships. This imbalance of power is creating significant stress in many marriages. One extensive study of American couples, by Philip Blumstein and Pepper Schwartz, pointed out that inequality experienced by women was a primary reason for unhappiness and the break up of marriages. People we see in therapy whose marriages are failing frequently describe either an imbalance of power that makes intimacy impossible or a struggle for power that is consuming the relationship.

Many contemporary marriages are, at least in theory, partnership marriages founded upon the couple's shared belief that husbands and wives are equal partners in all aspects of life. The positive side of the Blumstein and Schwartz study is that equality and shared power was a significant reason given by those couples who enjoyed their relationships and were choosing to stay married.

Many couples who consciously want to live in a marriage that gives both partners equal rights struggle with social and psychological pressures to function in traditional hierarchical patterns. Partnership marriages take more work than traditional marriage and can create more open conflict. The resulting frustration can lead to internal pressure to retreat into traditional over/under types of relating. Either partner might find it easier to follow traditional patterns to avoid an immediate conflict. However, these frustrations can build up and cause dissatisfaction.

Sara, a legal assistant, and Jason, who worked for an overnight delivery company, lived together for eighteen months before deciding to marry, a decision they made after Sara had been pregnant for five months. They were committed to an egalitarian relationship and were able to find jobs that allowed them to share in the care of their son. However, making decisions about the care of their son became more and more difficult. Then, to their surprise, Jason's feelings began to change. Though he believed cognitively that child care should be shared by husbands and wives, Jason began to feel aggravated that he had to spend so much of his free time in child care. As he began to pull back Sara began to feel both angry at Jason and guilty about not spending more time with their son. They came to a counselor when they began planning for Sara to quit her job and she recognized the underlying resentment about the unfairness of such a plan. They became aware that "down deep" they both thought child care was "women's work."

There are several psychological reasons for supporting partnership marriages, even though they require the most work. One reason is because unequal status and power limit the depth of intimacy attainable in any relationship. Jason and Sara, mentioned above, had become increasingly more distant because of the power struggle. You can recognize from your own experience that it is difficult to experience intimacy with someone who is in a position to make decisions about your life. In relationships between employers and employees, coaches and players, lieutenants and privates, landlords and tenants, the parties rarely share deep levels of intimacy even if they are friendly. When the structures allow the other person to control your life, then you normally protect your innermost self from being known by that person. The result of socialization that makes husbands "head of the house" and women their helpers is a power imbalance that creates the same limits on intimacy. Marriages characterized by mutuality and equality have the most potential for intimacy.

Another reason for our commitment to partnership marriage is that hierarchical marriages can be destructive. Beyond limited levels of intimacy, the imbalance of power results in bitter struggles, injustice, resentment, hostility, and stunted growth for both partners. When one partner does not have equal power he or she often develops some type of problem as a way of expressing anger or trying to equalize power. Problems with sexual avoidance, irresponsible spending, addictions, and depression, for example, can be the result of power imbalance. In marital therapy we find that the spouse who feels powerless finds it difficult to give up behavior that creates conflict. The behavior is a way for the underpowered spouse, usually the woman, to try and establish a sense of power or control that would balance the relationship. On the other hand, couples who are committed to mutuality and equality have a much easier time finding solutions to their problems. Therefore, it serves the marriage well when partners are sensitive to imbalances of power and are intentional in their search for equality.

SHARED POWER:
A FAITH PERSPECTIVE

The primary reason we are committed to partnership marriages is not psychological, but theological. We believe that equal rights and shared power, expressed through mutual leadership and earned authority, represent the theological perspective of the Christian faith for marital relationships. Hierarchical marriages (in which the husband has authority while the wife is submissive) from our perspective are contrary to the good news of the Christian gospel. We do not believe that in our culture at this time in history "traditional marriage," in which husband is leader and wife is follower, is defendable as God's desire for male/female relationships. In marriage relationships that acknowledge the Christian faith as a guide, women should have the freedom to pursue life with equal rights and responsibilities.

To believe that males have a God-given right to be the boss as if they were created in some superior fashion, or have been given some natural authority over women, does not take the cultural captivity of scripture and tradition seriously. By cultural captivity, we mean the ways in which scripture expresses cultural perspectives that were valid for the centuries in which it was written. Searching for God's revelation relevant for our day demands a reexamination of scripture, looking beneath the cultural specifics to find the profound layers of truth that lead to deeper understandings of human possibility. We must be aware of how patriarchy and sexism continuously interfere with our understanding of the Redeemer's message. For the Christian couple the theological and spiritual reasons for pursuing equality are important. We now ask the question of scripture, "What did God intend for male/female relationships?"

We start with the creation stories. Through these stories our ancestors in the faith summed up their understandings of how the world came into being. They included, interestingly enough, answers to their questions about why there are two genders and how these two genders are to be connected.

In the Beginning Male and Female

In the first creation story (Gen. 1:1–2:4a) the earth is carefully and systematically created out of chaos. Earth and sky, land and sea, plants and animals are brought into existence. After everything else is finished God says,

> Let us make humankind in our image, according to our likeness . . .
> So God created humankind in his image, in the image of God he created them; male and female he created them. God blessed them, and God said to them, "Be fruitful and multiply, and fill the earth and subdue it; and have dominion over . . ." (Gen. 1:26–28)

Notice several truths revealed in these few verses:

- When God first began to imagine humankind, both male and female were included. The tellers of this story believed that from the beginning humans existed in both male and female form. Neither sex was created first, nor given rank or status in creation higher than the other.
- Both male and female were created in God's image. Here we have a significant statement of belief which claims that both sexes are created in God's own image. Each of us, regardless of gender, is a reflection of God's own self.
- The plural pronoun makes it clear that both male and female received God's blessing. They were equally special in God's heart and the recipients of God's love and grace.
- Both male and female were given the responsibility to be fruitful and multiply, to create family and community. This was not an assignment directed at the woman.

- Both male and female were given dominion over the earth, responsibility for taking care of this planet. This was not an assignment directed at the man.

No authority by one gender over the other is even suggested, much less built into the creation. The male is not established as the superior or dominant gender, nor given the assignment to rule over females. Male and female are equal in their essential humanness, spiritual peers with reference to their relationship with God, and partners in responsibility for creating family and taking care of the earth.

Becoming One Flesh

In chapter 2 we described the second creation story (Gen. 2:4b–25) in which a human being was created by God out of dust, placed in a garden, and instructed about which trees to harvest. As you remember, God became aware that something wasn't right—this person was alone. So God brought woman into being as "a helper as his partner." The story ends by describing that the man and woman "become one flesh." Though quite different than the first creation story, this story is also clear about the basic equality before God of female and male. Notice the following:

- Both male and female are created by God, communicating the same truth that the first creation story describes by having males and females created at the same time.
- The woman is "bone of my bones and flesh of my flesh" (Gen. 2:23), meaning that men and women are the same in their essential humanness. She is different, but made of the same stuff. She is also fully human, part of the "crown of creation."
- The woman is created to be a partner, not a secretary, housekeeper, or nurse. The words "a helper as his partner" translate two Hebrew words 'ezer kenegdo. The first comes from two roots: "to rescue" and "to be strong" and usually means "to help." The second word occurs only once and means "equal." So together they mean something like "a helper equal to," thus there is no suggestion of subservience in the text. In fact elsewhere in scripture the same word 'ezer describes God as the helper (see Psalms 33:20 and 70:5), so it obviously doesn't refer to an inferior or second-class being!

- They become "one flesh" (Gen. 2:24), which is not a concept that connotes a hierarchical relationship. "One flesh" does not suggest that either gender has "natural" superiority over the other, or has been given responsibility to rule over the other. On the contrary, "one flesh" connotes partnership, mutuality, and oneness that comes because humans are created in two forms that fit well together in overcoming loneliness.

The Loss of Partnership

But doesn't the Bible say that men should rule over their wives, you ask? Yes, this piece of the traditional answer to male/female relationships comes from the third chapter of Genesis, where we find the famous story about the snake talking Eve into eating the forbidden fruit. After God discovers what has happened, the consequences of human disobedience are announced. Among other things it was said to the woman, "Your desire shall be for your husband, and he shall rule over you" (Gen. 3:16). It is important to note that male dominance in this story is connected to human sinfulness and is not what God originally had in mind.

When writers argue for traditional marriage patterns by referring to this text, they often discuss this announced pattern of male dominance as if it were originally intended by God and should continue forever as the norm for marriage. From a Christian perspective, however, this ignores the work of Jesus Christ who makes it possible for believers to become "new beings," as the apostle Paul phrased it. As believers we have been "born again" and "transformed." Being forgiven for our sins gives us the potential, even the responsibility, to transform hierarchical patterns between males and females back into the pattern of equality and mutuality described in the creation stories as God's original intention. When males "lord it over" females, and females give in, they both are continuing the pattern which grew out of sinfulness rather than boldly working out their salvation and acting out their redemption by claiming the work of Christ who has "broken down the dividing wall, that is, the hostility between us" (Eph. 2:14).

"Subject" to One Another?

Much has been made of the verses in Ephesians which call women to "be subject to your husbands as you are to the Lord. For the husband is the head of the wife just as Christ is the head of the church" (5:22–23). These verses are often taken out of context and used by some authors to describe what they call "God's divine plan" for authority in the family, namely a chain of command hierarchical structure with the husband as the chief executive officer. Traditional interpretations often view these verses as focused on authority. This view ignores the larger purpose of Ephesians and the meaning of the word translated "be subject to."

A closer look reveals that the purpose of Ephesians is to teach that those who belong to Christ are different than other people in the Greco-Roman culture. How? Followers of Christ relate on the basis of mutual love and respect, not authority. The broader message being conveyed is stated in the first verse of this chapter, "Therefore be imitators of God, as beloved children, and live in love, as Christ loved us and gave himself up for us" (Eph. 5:1). The author continues then to discuss how Christians can "live in love," including concepts about husband/wife relationships.

When discussing marriage the author of Ephesians states as a starting principle (5:21) that partners "be subject to one another out of reverence for Christ." The word translated "be subject to" is not a word that means "be obedient to." There are words that mean to be obedient, to be sure and do what the authority tells you to do. Two of those words are used by the author in chapter 6 to describe the relationship of slaves to masters and children to parents. The author is careful not to use those words here because the focus is on carefully establishing the basis for a new type of relationship between husband and wife. The word used here can better be translated "be supportive of," "tend to the needs of," or "respect the needs and desires of." Because of the basic principles of humility and caregiving included in Christian love, husbands and wives are to serve each other as Christ served the church.

After establishing this basic principle of mutual support and care, the author interprets the point for both wives and husbands. Because women in that culture were already accustomed to submission, the author uses three short sentences to address the wife's side of "being subject to one another" (5:22–24). Then comes the radical message of this passage, which is not wives submitting to husbands, but husbands submitting to wives. The author uses seven sentences to describe how the husband should love his wife "as Christ loved the church and gave himself up for her." Obviously, acting as boss or "lording it over" is not the way Christ loved the church. Christ loved through sacrifice and working to empower the disciples. The author suggests that "husbands should love their wives as they do their own bodies," again showing that care and respect are the operative principles.

EXERCISE: Draw a Picture of "One Flesh"
and/or "Subject to One Another"
We have now discussed two crucial verses about male/female relationships: Genesis 2:24, which declares that husband and wife "become one flesh" and Ephesians 5:21 that calls husbands and wives to "be subject to one another." For an interesting experience in grasping what these verses convey about male/female relationships, find some paper, pencils, or crayons and draw a picture of what these two phrases mean.

Notice how difficult it is to image through drawings that these words mean the male is to be dominant and the female submissive. Your picture will probably symbolize the mutuality and equality so foundational to these passages of scripture. Save your drawing; perhaps it will serve as a visual motivation for bringing more mutuality into your relationship.

Earlier in Ephesians we find more evidence that leader/follower is not the structure being recommended for Christian marriage. The author pleads with the readers "to lead a life worthy of the calling," a process described as living "with all humility and gentleness, with patience, bearing with one another in love, making every effort to maintain the unity of the Spirit in the bond of peace" (4:2–3). Does this sound like a manifesto for hierarchical relationships between Christians? Of course not. The radical message of the gospel is that brothers and sisters in Christ are called to relate with equality and mutuality. After all, Paul has already told us in Galatians 3:28 that in Jesus Christ there is neither male nor female. Marriage is between a brother and sister in Christ and is no different than any other relationship between Christians.

THE POWER STRUGGLE

Cultural stereotypes of women (too emotional, not good at math and science, good at taking care of children, and so forth) contribute to psychological pressures that influence women both consciously and unconsciously to view themselves as less important and powerful than males. In our culture, the attainment of a "voice" is more difficult for women than for men. By "voice" we mean to be taken seriously, to be heard and recognized as contributors, to be respected as perceptive and intelligent, to be seen as complete persons with an opinion and a vote. Authority in our society is generally granted to males. A wife may have grown up questioning whether it is appropriate for her to share authority with a male. These ingrained ways of seeing the world, which influence to some degree the worldview of most people (both male and female), color the fabric out of which your marriage is woven.

We must take a closer look at the meanings and dynamics of power. Power means the ability or agency to have an impact on something or someone, the capacity to affect change, or to be able to influence or force compliance. Power is both an external and internal reality. First, power is a social and political reality in our culture that is often enforced physically (rape, domestic violence) and socially (rituals, economics, traditions). That this culture grants men more power than women is not a figment of our imagination.

Second, this cultural reality establishes a parallel psychological reality. Perceptions of power as experienced early in life from family of origin and in the wider culture have been internalized to some degree by both spouses. The realities of both a patriarchal society and the incorporation of these realities into your psychological frames of reference may influence the way both of you express power in your relationship. Gender differences here are important because we bring these frames of reference into the marriage.

Power Over

Males are more likely to be socialized to think of power as "power over," defined as the strength to control others. "Power over" has the connotation of dominance, boss, or lordship. Men are taught to compete for control, to be in the "over" position, to call the shots. In the masculine world, power is connected with hierarchical worldviews and authoritarian structures which teach males to compete for the top spot. In this worldview power is usually defined by size and strength to dominate, whether physical (fighting, football, wrestling, war) or economic (bigger paychecks, corporate power).

As a male you may have internalized to some degree the tradition that as a man you should have more power than women, specifically power *over* women. You have been raised to function in hierarchical structures, seeking status in over/under relationships, and you will have to guard against bringing that same worldview into your marriage. Husbands are particularly vulnerable when the relationship is under stress, and these deeply ingrained constructions of reality insert themselves into their interactions. Suddenly, a couple is in a power struggle.

> Fred and Greta have been married four years, during which he has finished graduate school and begun a two-year residency. Greta is in the second and last year of graduate studies. Unexpectedly she became pregnant and with ambivalence shared the news with Fred. His response was negative, feeling that both their educational programs were threatened. To her surprise, he immediately began talking about an abortion. When she was hesitant he became angry and reminded her of their agreement that they would not have a child until she earned her degree and he finished the residency. By the third day he was telling her that she "had no choice" but to "live up to their agreements." She called a therapist on the fourth day, after he announced that he had made an appointment for her at a clinic. Though she was uncertain about her own feelings, she was clear in her resentment that Fred acted as if he had the right to make the decision. She was deciding to fight this imbalance of power and resist the loss of her rights, or as she said, "I'm digging in my heels on this one."

Even if you have consciously decided that males and females have equal rights and responsibilities, you may be influenced by your training to seek the "power over" position.

As a husband you may be tempted to relate to your wife as if gaining respect, even from her, would necessitate being in the dominant position, establishing a "power over" stance. You may want to remind yourself that even though she may succumb, she is not therefore increasing her admiration of you, but feeling sad that males are caught up in this search for power, angry at your immaturity, and feeling more distant and less intimate with you. Over time this sense of distance can become alienation, a deep conviction that intimacy with you is impossible. She may assume that you don't want intimacy because she understands romantic love as caring for another in ways that call for empathy, mutuality, and justice.

Some argue that women like men to be strong and powerful. When this is true, however, the strength which women admire is not strength that is expressed by dominating a mate. The power that she can respect is strength that is used "on behalf of" those in need and those who are oppressed.

Underpowered

If "power over" is at one extreme of power possibilities, then at the other extreme we have what Carrie Doehring calls "underpowered." Women tend to have lower self-esteem, are hesitant to be assertive, and passive in expressing needs—even believing that their needs are not as important as those of males. The wife is the most likely person in a marriage to have her power taken away. Or, given the socialization of women to be submissive and obedient, a wife may tend to underfunction with her power by either discounting it or surrendering it all together.

A woman may function in a given situation as if the male should make a decision, even though at conscious levels both know the female has more experience with this type of situation. A wife may expect, or wait for, the husband to make decisions, or defer to his ideas. Later either or both may resent the process—her for giving up power, and him for feeling pressured to be the decision maker.

Since women usually are taught to avoid conflict and confrontation, it can be difficult for women to exercise power. Women often fear that if they confront the imbalance of power they will destroy the relationship. Being abandoned by someone they care for is very risky, so they often hide or suppress their frustration at being in the "under" position.

If you are a woman, you may want to guard against functioning as if you were "underpowered," as if you did not have the knowledge, skills, experience, and intuitive awareness that, in fact, you do possess. You may have been taught to protect the male's esteem by letting him function (or letting him think he is functioning) as the leader whether or not he knows how to do so in a given situation. This internal pressure often comes from family stories about gender roles that have been impressed on either or both partners.

Laura was advancing quickly up the corporate ladder in the controller's office of an expanding holding company. Her skills were admired by peers and supervisors. She was working hard by day and studying many hours at night in order to pass qualifying professional exams. Sam was in transition, having left one vocation (which he had found unfulfilling) and working in a sales position while considering other vocational possibilities. They entered marriage counseling to deal with the stress created in their relationship by her heavy study schedule and workload and his frustration at finding a fulfilling vocation. Their major concern was his outbursts of anger, frequently expressed around his failure to follow through on his commitments to family maintenance chores such as preparing meals, taking care of the dogs, and cleaning the house.

In an individual session, Laura expressed her concern that Sam's anger and resistance to his share of the chores was his response to her rapid vocational success. She was particularly concerned about disparity in earnings since her salary was more than twice that of Sam's. She wondered if she should decline the promotion currently on the table and considered purposefully failing the next exam in order not to appear smarter than Sam. She was deeply afraid that his anger would lead toward a divorce. She clearly stated that if such occurred it would be her fault because her success "took away his role as the provider" and "embarrassed him before his friends."

Laura's family story was traditional and she remembered her mother's choice to protect her father's "male ego." Her parents had both been teachers, but her mother had turned down a coveted principal's position because she thought it would make Laura's father jealous and threaten the relationship. This sense of "men first," as Laura called it, was strongly entrenched in her family story.

It was hard for Laura to feel OK about her personal accomplishments because they seemed from her traditional perspective to be threatening to a male who was important to her. Her hesitation, even fear, is understandable. Most women are raised to shun power, and may feel that to exercise power will result automatically in conflict, loss of intimacy, and even abandonment.

As a wife, this surrender of power means that you do not allow yourself to be accountable for the power which you do possess. You give up opportunities to contribute to the marriage. Such surrender of power might be pleasing to a "power over" husband, but will be frustrating to a husband who is seeking mutuality and shared power. In either case, intimacy is compromised, as in the case of Laura and Sam mentioned above.

> Careful assessment revealed that Sam's behavior was an expression of frustration over his perceived failures. He felt he had wasted time pursuing a vocation that he did not like and was depressed over his present indecision. Consequently, he projected anger he felt toward himself onto the marriage. Yes, he identified some irritation that he was not "being taken care of" at home, but he knew that was connected to his past and dismissed this feeling as inappropriate. Actually, he enjoyed Laura's success and was proud of her accomplishments. His verbal support was genuine, but she had to overcome socialized ideas about power in order to accept his affirmation.

By silencing your voice, hiding behind excuses of inadequacy, or working to protect the male ego, you fail to offer your real self to the relationship.

Traditional marriages, with men as head of the family, are problematic for a number of reasons already stated, but another has to do with the possibility of injustice. When one person is given the power to make final decisions for other people, then acting justly becomes more difficult. Injustice is often the result of misused power. As the saying goes, "power corrupts," and having power often tempts marriage partners to abuse this power by acting in ways that are not just. The more power held by either partner, the more likely that partner is to behave toward the other unjustly. Though the person who is in the subordinate position is more likely to be the victim of injustice, the dominant partner is also in a losing situation because intimate loving is only possible in the context of mutual relationships. We will explore the justice issue further in chapter 7.

Empowerment/Power on Behalf Of

Because women, generally speaking, have not openly competed with men for "power over," some observers have assumed that women do not possess the personality traits that allow them to exercise power. Recent studies of women expand the meanings of power and challenge this assumption that women are powerless (see Jordan, et al., in "For Further Reading" at the end of this chapter). They use phrases such as "power with" and "power on behalf of" to describe the type of power with which women have historically felt comfortable. Women are raised to be more collaborative in their relationships and are not as tempted to function unilaterally. Rather than functioning in "power over" processes, such as making unilateral decisions for the family, they will more likely want to involve husbands in consultative discussions prior to making decisions, an expression of "power with."

Between "overpowering" and "underpowered" on the continuum of power lies this fertile middle ground of "empowerment." Empowerment describes the use of power toward the goal of promoting the growth and development of each partner and the relationship. "Power with" is used to describe power expressed through a unified front, power which is shared. "Power on behalf of" is the capacity to empower and influence in ways that are not coercive or forceful, but enables others to find their own power. Such empowerment does not sacrifice the self of the empowering person.

EXERCISE: Uncovering Your Story

Our thoughts and feelings about power and authority in marriage are significantly influenced by what we experienced in the homes where we grew up and what we heard within our larger environment. Frequently these influences are not clear to us because we have not taken time to explore them. If you and your partner want to be more aware of the personal history that affects the ways each of you conceptualize and express power, take time to explore your stories and bring to consciousness your early models for male/female relationships, particularly in husband/wife relationships. In leisurely dialogue, explore the following questions:

• What did you learn while growing up from family and com-

munity about power and authority as it should be expressed between husbands and wives?
- Which gender has the "right" to make decisions? Why?
- Which gender is the most "logical," has the most "common sense," knows the most about how the world functions? Why?
- How have you been influenced by your family of origin and the wider culture to think of chores and tasks to be done by husbands and wives?
- What did you hear from your church and the Christian community about power and authority between husbands and wives?

Power is not inherently evil, though all of us are tempted to use power demonically. Power can be used in ways that are constructive or destructive. We assume that "power over" and "underpowered" are destructive within marriage. "Power with," "power on behalf of," and empowerment are the only legitimate expressions of power between spouses. Both women and men have the ability to use their power on behalf of others, to find fulfillment in empowerment.

BLESSED is the marriage in which both partners
seek to empower the other.

SHARED POWER:
AUTHORITY AND LEADERSHIP

In marriage enrichment events the question will often arise, "Well, if you have different ideas about something and can't reach a decision, who should decide?" Behind this question is usually the assumption that somebody has to be "in charge." The person asking this question will argue that all groups must have a leader, someone in authority to make the final decisions. This person will often ask the specific question, "Doesn't someone have to be the leader and take command?" The answer expected is "yes," with the further assumption, given our cultural expectations, that this leader will be the husband. These concerns about authority and leadership speak to the issue of power. If the legitimate expressions of power in marriage are "power on behalf of" and "power with" (rather than "power over" or "underpowered"), how does power get expressed?

Earned Authority

Authority means the right to decide or direct. A person who has "power over" usually has the authority to decide for others what their life is going to be like. Because this authority is backed by "power over" dynamics (such as physical force and economic power), this authority may be used against a partner, or in spite of a partner's needs and best interests. Between Christian partners such "power over" authority is not appropriate. Neither partner "wears the pants" (notice the gender bias in this phrase) in the family—in the sense that one has by nature more authority than the other. The authority we think appropriate to the love suggested by the gospel is mutual authority, authority which is earned and is activated only when freely given from one partner to the other.

At times one partner will need to function as the representative authority on behalf of the partnership. This partner will be acting out "earned authority" granted in a particular situation because he or she has demonstrated through experience, interest, knowledge, and/or expertise that he or she can best decide for, or act on behalf of, the couple. The partner granting such authority does so freely, trusting that the authority will be used in the best interests of each partner and the relationship. Earned authority is not expressed as "power over" the partner but as "power on behalf of" both the partner and the relationship.

> Shannon has developed extensive knowledge and skill in buying and selling stock. Her husband Juwan is not interested in economics nor financial information. He does not feel comfortable working with the mechanics of the stock market. They have mutually decided that because of her ability working the stock market, she should invest her disposable income, their IRAs, and a portion of his pension moneys. He has given her the authority to manage his pension fund and IRA. She describes the days' activities but does not enlist his advice in decision making. When she is at her computer making trades or on the phone with her broker, she is functioning as the authority for both of them.

Representative Leadership

Leadership is identified often as a characteristic that the person in authority must exhibit. Often the concept of leadership becomes synonymous with the dynamics of control exercised by the person formally or informally in charge. Everyone else is identified as a follower, subject to the decisions and actions of the leader.

Leadership in a marriage, however, is a function which can be shared. When leadership means that a person with more knowledge, experience, time, energy, or appropriate personality characteristic takes the lead in dealing with a particular situation, that is an acceptable, even thoughtful, expression of that person's power "on behalf of." This is not hierarchical leadership, but leadership that is truly representational. It is leadership that is assigned in the context of mutuality and partnership. In expressing such leadership one partner is acting out authority earned by faithfulness in the relationship. Both spouses are clear about the assignment and trust that the best interests of each partner and the relationship will be considered.

> Jackie is a nurse who relates well to Paul's mother, a widow of sixteen years. Paul and his mother have never had a smooth relationship. She continues to treat him as a little boy and he continues to resist that dynamic through trying to prove himself to her. They are in perpetual conflict for many reasons that are not clear to either. When his mother needed more medical attention and probably a move from independent living into some type of retirement situation, Paul asked Jackie to take major responsibility for relating to his mother and making arrangements. At his suggestion, Jackie has taken the lead. She is the one talking calmly through the alternatives, communicating with Paul's two brothers who live elsewhere, and taking Paul's mother to visit retirement centers. This leadership role is helpful for everyone involved. Paul has taken on some of Jackie's other normal routine so that she is not overly burdened during this period of time.

Couples must struggle to generate their own models and images for mutuality and shared power. One area of everyday living that challenges us to share power is the process of making decisions.

SHARED POWER:
DECISION MAKING

Relating in an egalitarian manner can be frustrating because it takes more time, energy, and serious communication. This can lead to anger, hardened positions, and finally a sense of stalemate. Often the pattern of communication changes to see who can "win" (gain power over) instead of mutual loving. Our experience is that when couples are unable to reach either consensus or compromise it is usually because the anger has inhibited their ability to search more thoroughly for solutions that respect the ideas and feelings of each partner. Instead of moving into a power struggle, we suggest you declare that conversation a "tie game" or a "hung jury" and end the decision-making process for the moment. Then at another time, using enhanced communication skills (see chapter 3), you can assess your differences and search for new clues which would enable you to find a mutually satisfying answer.

At times, of course, partners have entirely different value systems, personal experiences, and philosophies of life which lead to a legitimate stalemate. Their personal stories are so dissimilar around the issue at hand that consensus seems impossible and compromise uncomfortable. What now? Let us suggest several next steps besides destructive conflict or having one partner claim the power position and demand authority to make the decision.

Taking Turns

In the long run, some couples find that taking turns making decisions about stalemates shares the power and authority in the marriage. This is what we teach children, isn't it? Put a list on the refrigerator that keeps track of whose turn it is to make a decision when no mutually satisfying decision can be reached. Many couples have found that this process reduces conflict when deciding where to eat, which movie or TV program to watch, where to go and what to do on vacation, or what color to paint the family room.

Consultation

Seek a professional consultant who has expertise in the area of disagreement. If the argument is over financial matters, for example, a

IT TAKES TWO

financial institution (your local bank, investment firm, tax consultant) can provide a financial advisor with whom you can consult. Books, videos, relevant organizations, and other sources provide information and options that can change the perspectives of one or both partners and inform your decision. One couple who constantly argued over discipline issues for their four-year-old son were willing to seek consultation from a child psychologist.

Marriage Enrichment Groups

If you are in a support group with other married couples, explore with them the "stuck point" that is creating controversy in your marriage. Other couples will have creative ideas about both the content of your discussion and the process by which you are trying to make a decision.

Marriage Therapy

Many couples have found creative help from a few sessions with a competent therapist. A therapist can help you identify the reasons why the decision-making process has broken down and assist you in thinking through other possibilities. Reaching a stalemate may signal several concerns that need attention. A personal agenda from one partner's history might be affecting the way in which that partner is conceptualizing the problem. Or, the process by which you are striving toward a decision might be in need of an overhaul. A therapist can help you identify and repair the weak link in your decision-making process or help you adopt a whole new process.

Warning: Money is a key ingredient in power, or as one sweatshirt message has it, "The Golden Rule: The One With the Gold Makes the Rules." When one partner makes all, or most of, the money, that partner is tempted to function as if the money confers power. This may be acted out in providing an allowance for the other partner. But when one is given an allowance, it is obvious that the money does not belong to the partnership, but to the earner. The more unbalanced the earning power in a marriage, the more intentional the partners must be that the money does not become the source of a power imbalance and the resulting decrease in intimacy.

SHARED POWER:
DIVISION OF LABOR

Another test for couples who strive for shared power is the issue of dividing up who does what. Being married, particularly if there are children, means maintaining a living space and attending to those daily processes which allow a family group to function: preparing food, keeping the living space in decent order, dealing with insurance, filing taxes, making repairs, paying bills, finding presents for the family, planning celebrations, and emptying the garbage.

Though progress has been made, research shows that the work (tasks, chores) necessary to maintain a family is still divided by gender in two ways: the wife spends about twice as much time on domestic work as the husband, even among those couples who are both employed outside the home; and who does what is still largely determined by sex-role stereotypes—that is, rather than sharing tasks husbands and wives are more likely to divide tasks on the basis of traditional perceptions of "woman's work" and "man's work." These findings suggest that sharing responsibility for maintaining the family has not been accomplished in most marriages.

What criteria does a couple use to decide who does what chore? There is no scriptural assignment of specific chores to women and men. Christian couples must base these decisions on the principles of shared power and authority, plus the commitment to equality and justice. From a practical standpoint the following criteria can be helpful:

Who has the time?

Time is available to each partner depending on work schedules and other commitments. These commitments may remain basically stable for long periods of time so that tasks can be assigned on a long-term basis. For other couples time is available in a seasonal pattern.

Shirley works as a bookkeeper for a small accounting firm during tax season. From January through April she often works ten to twelve hours a day and most Saturdays. During these four months her husband, Dennis, turns most of his after work responsibilities with the Boy Scouts over to his partner and increases the amount of time he is available for their school-age children and the number of tasks he takes on at home. The rest of the year she handles small bookkeeping chores at home and Dennis increases his avocational involvement with the troop. They have carefully worked out this schedule so that both are satisfied.

Who has the physical ability?

One partner may be strong enough to carry the box to the attic or bring the Christmas tree from the garage. During times of injury or illness, one partner may not have the physical strength or capability for certain functions.

Who has the interest?

One spouse may have a heavy emotional investment in some tasks while the partner is indifferent (planting flowers in the yard, keeping more extensive records than legally necessary, capturing events on film, keeping the storage space neatly organized). The spouse who needs a particular task done more thoroughly and in a particular way to feel satisfied may need to be the partner who carries out the task.

Who has the courage?

Who is willing to climb the ladder to clean the gutters, or confront the neighbor about the high volume on his CD player, or check in the middle of the night to see what made the noise downstairs?

Who has the knowledge and skill?

One partner may have the knowledge and ability to perform certain tasks with more expertise than the other.

Who doesn't mind?

If no positive criteria can be found, a couple can decide on the basis of who has the least negative feeling toward a particular task. For one partner that specific task may not be exciting, but doing it is basically "no problem."

Andy does not mind doing laundry. He does it in the "cracks" of his schedule and does not find it a nuisance. Judy, on the other hand, thinks of laundry as a major task and will use most of a day completing the work. Therefore, doing the laundry is usually Andy's assignment. To give another example, Judy is an excellent cook who can organize a meal quickly and efficiently. Because Andy has never learned how, cooking becomes an overwhelming event. Consequently Judy usually takes care of meals at home.

Whose turn?

When all else fails, taking turns at those things which no one likes (cleaning the bathroom, washing the dog) may be the fairest decision. A list on the refrigerator that shows who did what last month will allow a couple (and children) to keep track of these chores.

What's fair?

If one partner is feeling that he or she ends up with the heavier burden, he or she can feel legitimately that the marriage is unfair. If one partner is overcommitted to work or outside interests to the neglect of an equitable division of labor, then resentment begins to brew. What does justice call for? A couple who keeps the idea of fairness in mind and consciously applies this concept will find more sense of intimacy and fulfillment. After all, love "does not insist on its own way" (1 Cor. 13:5). Empowerment means that each partner is also working to learn other skills and gain further knowledge so that each individual can expand the number of maintenance processes for which he or she can take responsibility.

Warning: An equitable division of labor is more difficult when the man assumes on the basis of his socialization that he is to be taken care of by women. To the extent that the husband has been raised this way, to that extent will he be tempted to feel that what he doesn't want to do should be done by the women in his life, particularly his wife. At the same time, a woman brought up to believe that service is the highest good can easily move into self-giving that becomes self-sacrificial beyond what love calls for in a mutual relationship. This leads to an imbalance of power and the resulting loss of intimacy and vulnerability to injustice.

EXERCISE: What Are Your Criteria for Dividing Tasks?

Like most couples, you may not have intentionally established criteria for dividing tasks. Instead, your process of making decisions and dividing tasks may happen randomly or out of habit. Choose (on

IT TAKES TWO

the basis of ongoing conflict) several of the maintenance tasks. Discuss how the two of you made the decision about who would be assigned that task. Is your criteria based on traditional stereotypes about male/female roles and "rights" rather than criteria listed above? If your process of making assignments does not represent your commitment to participation in a journey of shared power and responsibility, take time to develop a different plan.

PATRIARCHY AND POWER

We have described from scripture and theology why we believe that Christian couples must be committed to shared power. In reality, of course, the history of marriage as an institution directed by the male as the dominant spouse and the "lord of his castle" is hard to overcome. Don't underestimate how these ideas impact how you and your spouse relate. This hierarchical model for marriage runs deep in the collective psyche of our culture and is transmitted by our institutions. Our basic life stories are often influenced by these traditions even when our cognitive choice is for partnership. Only in this century has the idea of partnership marriage, with emphasis on partnership, become an acceptable concept in our culture.

We take seriously the research that shows that gender inequality continues to oppress women. Though many positive changes have occurred, patriarchal cultural norms keep women in subservient positions. We must confront the reality that in our culture, males are given more power and authority than females. The idea that marriage is an over/under relationship with the male on top as boss and the woman underneath as servant/secretary/cook/domestic help is strong. Though our society has given up the idea, publicly at least, that men "own" women as another possession, husbands are often thought of as being the head of the house with all the trappings and prerogatives thereof. Women who are finding some equality and respect outside the home and marriage do not want to return to prison at night.

There are still those in the church, particularly on the "religious right," who believe that the male should be the head of the home and the wife submissive. They view the male as having within God's divine order the right and responsibility of leadership and protection of the wife who is privileged to be the follower and receive protection. Books promoting this neo-authoritarian view have sold thousands of copies and seminars supporting this view draw thousands of participants.

Your wedding, if held in a church, probably demonstrated the power differential between males and females still believed in by some faith traditions and local churches. You may have participated in a ceremony which unknowingly acknowledged the passing down of male power. Though vows are often more mutual than the traditional "love and obey," the service may have symbolized that the wife belongs to her husband. The groom may have entered the sanctuary from a door near the altar with the pastor or priest, symbolizing his closer association with God. The bride is brought to the groom, as if she belonged to him. The groom is not brought to the bride. She is accompanied down the aisle by her father rather than the mother or both parents. Why? Given the tradition of male ownership, particularly of female sexuality, women don't have the power to give women away. The question may have been asked by the presiding pastor or priest: "Who is giving the bride to this man?" and the father may have answered "I do," as if he were the owner and had the right to "give her away" to another man.

TRADITIONAL PATTERNS DIE SLOWLY

Were you tempted to skip this chapter because you perceive that you and your spouse are functioning in an egalitarian relationship? Don't be overconfident. Don't underestimate the influence of the hierarchical story about sex roles. We often see the power of unrecognized sex-role stereotypes and gender biases held by both males and females. Partners who value fairness and are committed to an egalitarian relationship are surprised by the extent to which their relationship can be invaded by traditional stereotypes. Our experience in both enrichment workshops and therapy sessions reveals how these assumptions can wreak havoc on a marriage without the partners realizing what is happening.

Patricia was already committed to pursuing an advanced degree when her relationship with Glen turned into a serious romance. By the time they considered marriage she was interviewing with several graduate schools. In premarital counseling they faced the issue of what it felt like to him to follow his wife's vocational goals. He was clear that, since he felt no particular vocational direction of his own, he would willingly accompany her anywhere and find work. She accepted a fellowship in a university that moved him away from where he was raised. After a three-year program a post-doctoral scholarship became available in a state even further from his home. He claimed that he was willing to go, but shortly after their arrival he became abusive and seriously depressed. He hated his job, the weather, and the distance from his father who was in a health crisis. In therapy he confessed his resentment that her career had been predominant and "taken him so far from his roots." He wanted to follow their mutual covenant, but was aware that his deeper sense of male entitlement was stronger than he imagined.

Couples committed to an egalitarian relationship can easily slip into hierarchical patterns of relating. Heightening your awareness of these ingrained concepts enables you to be on guard for ways in which they seek to poison your relationship.

Given the power issues between males and females, it is not surprising that a common cause of conflict between spouses is the struggle for or against control. Most men have been taught to compete for control and may be functioning in a way to try and gain control. At the same time they may resist any action on the part of their wife that leaves them feeling she is in control. Many women, of course, are sensitive to their rights to be equal and are both striving for equality and resisting their husband's attempts at control. Many arguments take place, therefore, not because of the specific event but because of the underlying concern about being controlled. In the last chapter we examined how to deal with the anger generated by these power struggles and other threats.

A couple wanting to struggle toward, or work to maintain an intimate marriage must consistently evaluate whether power is shared, because our culture, our histories, and our individual desires are constantly pushing us toward either dominant or subordinate roles within the relationship. If either partner feels that the other has either "moved over" or "moved under," he or she must confront that imbalance and invite the other to join in assessment of what happened and in making covenants to restore shared power. Such confrontation is typically more difficult for women who have been socialized to accept the subordinate position and fear that confrontation may result in the loss of relationship. A commitment to confront this imbalance not only means that the woman must confront the male for "moving over," but that the male must confront the female for "moving under" or vice versa.

EXERCISE: Consciousness Raising

Partners who heighten their awareness of the inherent imbalance of power in our culture will be more sensitive to this imbalance when it creeps into their relationship. Reading feminist literature in the social sciences, particularly in psychology and marriage and family studies, will sensitize you to the ways in which these beliefs and traditions influence your relationship. A deeper understanding of the Christian story about mutuality and justice in relationships between members of the family of God will challenge you to confront the imbalance of power in your relationship and to express love through justice with each other. Search out imbalances of power and make covenants (see chapter 8 for instructions) toward shared power.

FOR FURTHER READING

Blumstein, Philip, and Pepper Schwartz. *American Couples*. New York: William Morrow and Co., 1983.

Doehring, Carrie. "Life-Giving Sexual and Spiritual Desire." *Journal for Pastoral Theology* 4 (summer 1994): 49–69.

Freedman, R. David. "Woman, A Power Equal to Man." *Biblical Archaeology Review* 9, no. 1 (Jan/Feb, 1983): 56–58.

Jordan, Judith V. et al. *Women's Growth In Connection*. New York: The Guilford Press, 1991.

Rampage, Cheryl. "Power, Gender, and Marital Intimacy." *The Association for Family Therapy* 16 (1994): 125–137.

Van Leeuwen, Mary Stewart, ed. *After Eden*. Grand Rapids: William B. Eerdmans, 1993.

Wilfong, Marsha M. "Genesis 2:18–24." *Interpretation: A Journal of Bible and Theology* 42, no. 1 (January 1988): 58–63.

six

IF THIS IS SO MUCH FUN,
WHY DON'T WE DO IT MORE OFTEN?
The Joy of Sexual Intimacy

The phrase "sexual union" usually refers to intercourse. In a deeper sense, sexual union refers to the intimacy that can be felt in the depth of an ecstatic sexual encounter. Within a sexual encounter it is possible to experience an almost indescribable sense of connectedness and communion. For this reason we celebrate our sexuality and its contribution to intimate marriage as one of God's special gifts.

Our sexuality is a constant reminder that we are relational beings. We need another person to complement our sexuality, to be the recipient of our love and to offer love in return. The Hebrew scriptures acknowledge the potential for expressing deep love and experiencing intimacy through our sexuality.

> Let your fountain be blessed,
> and rejoice in the wife of your youth,
> a lovely deer, a graceful doe.
> May her breasts satisfy you at all times;
> may you be intoxicated always by her love.
> (Proverbs 5:18–19)

The Song of Solomon includes romantic, sexually explicit poetry that captures the passionate longing and desire that can exist between lovers.

> Upon my bed at night
> I sought him whom my soul loves. (3:1)
> . . . .
> I am my beloved's,
> and his desire is for me.
> Come, my beloved,
> let us go forth into the fields, . . .
> There I will give you my love.
> (7:10–12)

Sexuality is an inescapable, integral aspect of being human. Our identity cannot be separated from our physical existence, which includes our sexuality. To be human is to be sexual. We don't come any other way. From birth our identity unfolds as a sexual being, specifically as male or female. We cannot choose to be nonsexual without risking psychological and spiritual harm. Sexuality is one aspect of the mystery of our personality. The uniqueness that stamps your existence as different from any other person includes the particular way in which you are masculine or feminine. Therefore, one aspect of the fascination that your partner feels toward your unique self has to do with your sexuality.

On the basis of TV, movies, and water cooler conversation, one would think that everyone in this culture is having sex all the time and enjoying it thoroughly. But recent research suggests that married adults are not having as much sex as advertised. The "Sex in America" survey conducted by the University of Chicago found that one-third of the couples surveyed have sex only several times a year or none at all, while another third have sex only several times a month. The sexual encounters dramatized on film are exaggerated in frequency and intensity compared to real-life experience for most couples.

After a few years of marriage a typical couple experiences a cooling off period in their sexual relationship. They have not stopped having or enjoying sexual encounters, but these encounters are less frequent and often less passionate. Being creatures of habit, we often get trapped by routine and become vulnerable to boredom. Many couples in therapy and in marriage enrichment events are looking for the spark of passion that once energized their sexual encounters. Keeping sexual passion alive in long-term relationships is an important ingredient in attaining sexual intimacy.

This chapter seeks to describe the attitudes and behaviors that can lead a couple into sexual intimacy. We use the phrase "sexual encounter" to describe any sexual interaction between partners—from holding hands and winking across the room, to kissing, caressing, and sexual intercourse. We do not use the phrase "having sex" because it connotes only sexual intercourse, and intercourse is not necessary in every sexual encounter to experience sexual intimacy. When we want to refer specifically to intercourse, we will identify it as such.

THE CHRISTIAN FAITH
AND SEXUALITY

The history of the Christian tradition is well known for its negative perspective on sex. Human sexuality was very threatening to some of the early church theologians. They divided the creation into two parts: the spiritual and the material. Because sexuality is so obviously connected to the body, they assigned sexuality to the material world. Sexuality, therefore, was perceived as a threat to our spiritual nature. They blamed the Evil One for the existence of sexual temptation, believing that sexual desire was punishment for human disobedience.

As a result of this negative interpretation, sexuality became something Christians had to overcome. Those Christians who refrained from any sexual function such as masturbation and intercourse were perceived as being more spiritual. Those who could keep themselves from even thinking or feeling about sex were seen as the most spiritual of all. Though much progress has been made, you may have been raised in a church and family that avoided the subject or portrayed it negatively, as if God was upset that humans are sexual.

Sexuality and Creation

From a Christian perspective our entire self, including our sexuality, was brought into being by the Creator. Sexuality is not the result of a blunder by God, but part of God's plan from the beginning. We were brought into existence as male and female. Surely, being created in the image of God means that our essential humanness reflects God's being, which means that somehow sexuality is part of God reflected in our existence.

Scripture is clear that sexuality is part of that which God purposefully created. In the first creation story God observed all that had been made, including sexuality, and said "it was very good" (Gen. 1:31). When the apostle Paul tells Timothy that "everything created by God is good, and nothing is to be rejected, provided it is received with thanksgiving" (1 Tim. 4:4) our sexuality is included.

The second creation story supports the conclusion that our capacity for sexual pleasure was purposefully created and blessed by God. The man and woman "become one flesh" (Gen. 2:24), which means, among other things, that they shared their love in sexual union. This passage ends with the important message that though naked, the man and woman "were not ashamed" (Gen. 2:25). In this creation story sexuality and sexual attraction did not create a sense of shame and embarrassment.

One purpose of our creation as male and female, of course, is procreation, to "be fruitful and multiply" as the first creation story puts it (Gen. 1:28). But in the second creation story procreation is not mentioned as a reason for the creation of two genders. The concern in this story, as we pointed out in chapter 1, was God's desire to overcome loneliness. God did this, according to this story, by creating companions who were essentially the same, but also complemented one another sexually. Sexual encounters have the capacity to help us overcome loneliness. As male and female "become one flesh" they find a meaningful expression of love and community within an intimate relationship. Sexual capability is one of God's gifts to us and we can offer our joyful participation in loving sexual encounters as both a gift to our spouse and a response to God's wonderful creation. Imagine God smiling in delight when you are experiencing the sexual excitement and satisfaction that God envisioned from the beginning.

Sexuality and Spirituality

Sexual encounters can be sacramental. That is, they can represent divine/human interaction. A meaningful sexual encounter that brings spouses into deep communion with each other has the capacity to put us in touch with the transcendent nature of our existence. A passionate sexual experience, particularly orgasm, can explode our sense of finite limitation and create feelings which are not unlike a mystical experience. Sexual intimacy can enhance our sense of the presence of God and make us aware of God's blessing on the relationship.

Throughout Christian history there have been those who wanted to separate the physical from the spiritual, but the marvelous experience of orgasm with a loved and loving partner can reach beyond physical pleasure to become a profound spiritual experience. In the same moment we can experience the heights of physical ecstasy and the depth and breadth of spiritual oneness. This capability should convince us that procreation was not the only, not even the primary, purpose for our creation as two sexes.

> BLESSED are the couples who imagine God
> viewing their sexual encounters with a smile.

The biblical use of the term "to know" as a synonym for sexual intercourse in the Hebrew scriptures is not simply a polite way of dealing with this subject, for the Hebrews were not puritanical. Rather, the use of this verb hints at the deeper emotional and spiritual possibilities for intimacy within sexual encounters. Indeed, sexual intercourse is the "deepest" we can encounter a loved, committed partner, thereby providing potential for a profound connection with our spouse. Sexual intimacy can be a major contributor to the overall intimacy which is possible in a marital relationship. Sexual experience at its best colors everything else with the sense of special privilege and commitment.

"To know" refers also to self-discovery in sexual encounters. Within the most intimate sexual encounters, a person finds aspects of self that were heretofore unknown. Who you are as a person, particularly your identity as a male or female, becomes more clear as the uniqueness of your sexuality is explored and expanded in the context of sexual experience.

Sexuality and Equality

Scripture describes sexual desire and need on the part of both male and female. Furthermore, both are allowed to express these needs and take initiative toward their lover. The apostle Paul was not very supportive of sexual involvements because of his expectation of the immediacy of Christ's return. But when he did speak of marital sexual encounters he was committed to equality and mutuality. He wrote,

> The husband should give to his wife her conjugal rights, and likewise the wife to her husband. For the wife does not have authority over her own body, but the husband does; likewise the husband does not have authority over his own body, but the wife does. Do not deprive one another except perhaps by agreement for a set time, to devote

yourselves to prayer, and then come together again, so that Satan may not tempt you because of your lack of self-control. (1 Cor. 7:3–5)

Notice that there is no suggestion that the man's needs are a priority, nor that the woman must meet these needs without thought to her own sexual desires. The clear message is that mutual pleasure is the norm for Christians.

> BLESSED is the couple who excitedly respond
> to each other's sexual desires.

Even with his uncertainties about the end time, Paul spoke in favor of sexual pleasure in marriage. He obviously did not believe that sexual involvement would hinder spiritual growth, nor participation in the coming kingdom of God.

THE CONTEXT FOR SEXUAL INTIMACY

A haphazard act of sexual intercourse can occur in almost any context (even marriage). Many people "have sex" or "do it" outside of a special relationship for the physical gratification, or to try and make some emotional connection. In marriage it often happens as part of the routine or out of a sense of duty. But joyful sexual intimacy, the coming together of two committed selves in an erotically pleasurable encounter, occurs intentionally in the context of a loving relationship marked by the following characteristics.

Trust

Given the degree of vulnerability called for in the process of a meaningful sexual encounter, trust is a basic necessity for sexual intimacy. Enjoyable and fulfilling sexual encounters occur in the context of freedom and spontaneity, which is not possible without the foundation of trust. Trust includes the certainty that you will not be used, abused, hurt, ridiculed, or abandoned. The depth of sexual intimacy possible is directly proportional to the degree of trust within the relationship.

Moving into sexual intimacy cannot happen without some risk of making mistakes, feeling awkward or embarrassed, confronting ignorance, and misinterpreting the partner. Few events leave us more exposed than a genuine sexual encounter. Trusting that our partner will not ridicule or make fun of us is crucial.

> Dianne grew up with a mother who was constantly critical of anything she tried to do. Consequently, Dianne developed into a cautious person who found it scary to try anything new. Now she wants to express her love for Samuel through sexual pleasure, but is so fearful of making a mistake that she avoids any attempts at sexual experimentation. She is embarrassed because she feels so inadequate. She finds it difficult to risk learning something new because of her fear of failure. But Samuel is gentle and accepting, never critical of her, which allows her to develop the trust in him that makes a significant difference as she slowly risks exposing herself in lovemaking.

A primary aspect of trust is security in the commitment to exclusiveness within the marital relationship. A sense of faithful commitment to an exclusive relationship provides the context for complete giving and receiving of one's sexual self.

Safety

One aspect of trust that is particularly important to women is physical safety. Many women have experienced forced participation in sexual interaction. Those who haven't know about the threat and fear of invasion and violation. This anxiety needs to be overcome if a woman is to experience desire and spontaneity in sexual encounters. Vulnerability and openness in a sexual encounter can only be expressed in the context of a covenant of trust that lends certainty to the belief that "I will not be violated." She needs to know that regardless of the intensity of passion generated, the sexual encounter always includes a commitment to protect her from force, and grants her control over what happens. She must have the freedom to direct or stop the proceedings if she becomes physically pained or emotionally uncomfortable. She must trust that her partner believes that sexual pleasure is to be given and received, not forced and taken. This is not only an issue for women, because men also fear demand and ridicule in sexual encounters. Men have connected body image with self-esteem and can feel embarrassed and discounted when teased or when unable to perform up to expectations.

Mutuality

When a couple has established trust, each can relax and know that sexual encounters will be mutual. Neither partner will use physical or psychological force. Freedom will characterize all sexual initiatives so that each partner has the freedom to participate or not. The desires of either partner can be expressed openly, but each willingly accepts those situations when the other partner is not interested or able to participate in a sexual encounter. This commitment protects either partner from feeling used, or worrying that satisfaction of physical urges will become more important to the partner than the ethic of mutuality. A particular sexual encounter might be entered into by choice, of course, with the desires of one partner being primary—but only when both partners agree on this purpose.

Since many of us were socialized to assume that male sexual needs are a priority and that males have the dominant roles and responsibilities, males may find themselves tempted to function in a demanding manner, even when they are consciously committed to equality. Husbands can identify and resist explicit or implicit tendencies toward "power over" responses.

Women, on the other hand, can resist tendencies toward automatic submission, a role many were raised to connect with being feminine. Assuming that the male's needs are primary and that he has the right to direct lovemaking may lead you, as the wife, toward passivity, inhibiting communication about your desires and dampening your expression of passion.

Some women have also learned manipulative ways of using sexuality in light of the intensity of male sexuality. Using sex as a tool to gain leverage rather than meeting needs through direct communication (see chapter 3) gets in the way of sexual intimacy.

Self-giving and Receiving

Believing that God's love is freely given through grace gives us an important model for loving each other. An ideal sexual encounter, one that contributes to the sense of intimacy, is one in which we give our-selves openly and completely to our partner. This giving of ourselves represents the self-giving of God and sends a clear message about our love.

Self-giving includes making our whole sexual self—body, mind, and spirit—totally available. We are our spouse's to enjoy, trusting that he or she will receive our sexual self as a gift, an expression of our love. When our partner feels that one of our primary goals in a sexual encounter is to make her or him feel special, he or she will feel more responsive and experience more intimacy. Giving is most easily acceptable when it is nondemanding—that is, without expectation of a specific response. When our partner is tired, depressed, or preoccupied, we can give our sexual self with the hope that he or she will feel free to receive without expectation of giving in return.

Intimate sexual encounters also include receiving, which reflects God's loving acceptance of us. Each spouse can learn that making love includes receiving the partner's sexual self and acts of lovemaking. If depleted in some way, it is important to know that lovemaking can be received without obligation for specific responses. Such receiving is a way of giving pleasure and expressing love.

Giving and receiving are both enjoyable, and basic to sexual inti-macy. The couple who is free to give and receive in this manner can en-gage in meaningful sexual encounters more frequently because they do not have to feel the same level of sexual energy. One partner can be en-ergized to give and the other willing to simply receive. Each is trusting that there will be no further demand and both able to enjoy a loving and pleasurable encounter.

Respecting the Need for Distance

Regardless of the quality of sexual encounters, there are times when a partner needs distance rather than closeness. Times of stress, illness, preoccupation, depression, tiredness, dissatisfaction, or conflict within the relationship can make a spouse disinterested in any physical close-ness during a particular period of time. Respecting this need for dis-tance makes it possible for each partner to simply state this need rather than choosing distancing behaviors (eating onions, not showering, not shaving, going to bed early or late, starting an argument) that interrupt the larger fabric of intimacy.

When a partner's need for time alone is encouraged with tender regard for the necessity of self-maintenance, then the overall intimacy of the marriage is enhanced. The partner who asks for space can affirm the relationship by speaking specifically about her or his anticipated return: "I am not abandoning you, nor is being with you something I don't like. I just need some space at the moment, but will return and share what I can about myself." This is the kind of reassurance that maintains the sense of intimacy and trust.

ENHANCING SEXUAL INTIMACY

Over the years, both in therapeutic settings and in marriage enrichment events, we have listened to couples describe frustrations about their sexual relationship. They desired sexual intimacy but were not being successful in attaining this goal. When they analyzed the reasons for their frustration, and chose new behaviors, the most creative changes took place in the following categories:

Having Fun

Couples who play and have fun together enjoy sexual encounters. In our busy lives we often forget to play. How long has it been since you have been dancing, walked in the park, taken a picnic to the lake, taken in a movie, visited the local museums, or bowled a game? Nurturing the pleasant, relaxed, exciting, laughing aspects of life are important for setting the atmosphere in which we can feel playful in sexual encounters.

Creating Space for Sex

Prior to marriage you probably went to extremes in planning your schedules to include time with each other. You missed classes, took long lunches, turned down engagements, and skipped meetings because of the excitement and pleasure of being together. Your friends probably complained (with a grin) that they didn't see you very often. After settling into married life, however, your relationship assumed more normal proportions and energy was appropriately directed again toward other people and responsibilities. The danger, of course, is that we can lose this high degree of intentionality about creating private time in which romantic sexual encounters can occur. The loss of imagination about romantic adventures dampens the erotic potential.

At this moment do you have a special time planned in which you and your spouse could experience sexual intimacy? If not, why not? Busy schedules packed with obligations to job, church, and community, plus meeting children's needs, make it difficult for couples to find time to be alone. If a couple leaves sexual encounters to chance they may wait a long time between encounters. Couples who intentionally create space in which lovemaking can occur usually experience more sexual intimacy and fulfillment.

To recapture the magic, be intentional about claiming couple time. Date books in hand, choose some mornings or evenings that you can claim as your own. Married with children? Be imaginative.

- What about going to bed early on Friday night, getting a full night's rest, and having intimate time on Saturday morning behind a locked door while the school-age children watch cartoons and eat cereal?
- Can the children spend the evening with a friend or family member? Some couples trade child care on weekend evenings—the Johnson family keeps all the children this Friday night and the Wattleton family keeps them next Friday night—leaving the parents with an evening free from child care that can be spent any way they please in their own home or elsewhere.
- Churches who sponsor "Parents Night Out" programs in which child care is offered for four hours on a Friday evening provide a wonderful gift to couples with young children.
- Pay a young couple from your church to care for the children while you have a "getaway" weekend.

In short, the creative couple who wants to spend intimate time together can plan ahead. This means choosing each other over other events, turning down some social invitations, saying no to a meeting, finishing an assignment early, and cutting down on other commitments. Remember the power of the imagination! Be creative!

BLESSED is the spouse whose partner expresses
love through intentional romance.

Many sexual encounters come at the end of a long day filled with
energy-consuming functions that leave us with less emotional and
physical resources. Though sexual encounters when we are tired may
be meaningful, they are of a different type than those which take place
during high energy times. So when planning opportunities for romantic sexual encounters, pick times when you are both full of emotional and physical energy.

Enjoying the Pleasure of Touch

Most of us marry someone to whom we are physically attracted. We
experience sexual arousal in her or his presence and desire to touch
and be touched. These experiences of touch are exciting and pleasurable. During courtship touching becomes more intimate and we enjoy the exhilarating pleasures of caress. After the marriage gets under
way, however, the amount of time spent enjoying the pleasures of
erotic touch are often reduced by time constraints, tiredness, and preoccupation. The time frame between the initiation of a sexual encounter and the climax of intercourse may be shortened. Sadly, the
pleasure of foreplay gets jettisoned in favor of the more intense release
of orgasm.

BLESSED is the spouse whose partner enjoys
the pleasure of erotic touch.

Intercourse and orgasm, as important as they may be, cannot by
themselves provide a sense of sexual intimacy. God's gift of sexuality
is marked by our capacity to experience physical pleasure. If sexual encounters are to be experienced as romantic, as well as erotic, they will
be characterized by sensuous playtime. Enjoying your partner's sexual
self is one way of blessing your spouse. Several books are mentioned
at the end of the chapter which could guide you in this discovery.

Removing Intercourse from Its Pedestal
(Do You Have to Go All the Way?)

Sexual satisfaction in our culture, particularly for males, is usually equated with intercourse. Some couples develop an unspoken rule that every sexual encounter must move toward the grand finale—intercourse—followed, of course, by orgasm. A sexual encounter can be treated like a race in which the goal becomes the fastest way to intercourse—an approach which forgets all of the pleasurable possibilities between the first flirtation and coitus. There are times, of course, when a couple is mutually excited and concurs that moving quickly to intercourse is the most fulfilling choice, but more often than not we rush because of being too tired, or bored, and sexual encounters become perfunctory.

In therapy we frequently see couples whose dissatisfaction with their sexual relationship is directly related to maintaining this "all sex must lead to intercourse" concept. If she does not feel like being penetrated or he does not feel interested in or capable of maintaining an erection, then he or she will find a way to avoid a sexual encounter by ignoring the partner's signals, starting a fight, going to bed early or late, running an errand, or in some other way communicating, "I am not interested in being sexually close."

Couples who don't have to "go all the way" in every sexual encounter are free to enjoy whatever level of erotic encounter they need and want in a given situation. Why? Because they know that the partner will honor their disinterest in sexual intercourse and focus on the erotic possibilities in sexual pleasuring. Such freedom increases both quality and quantity of sexual encounters.

The freedom to have sexual encounters without intercourse makes it more likely that partners can respond meaningfully to sexual initiatives when one partner's sexual desires are low, such as during a time of stress. Focusing on the pleasure and intimate potential in lovemaking without intercourse is particularly helpful to the male who is impotent because of medicine, surgery, or stress, and the female who is experiencing infection, late stages of pregnancy, the weeks following birth, or stress.

BLESSED is the person who has a spouse
who likes to touch and cuddle.

Forgoing intercourse does not necessarily mean inhibiting orgasm. A couple who decides, because of the needs of either partner, to leave intercourse out of a particular sexual encounter may still experience the pleasures of orgasm. If past history or upbringing makes you think of this as masturbation and, therefore, a negative experience, reflect back on your theology of sex to recognize that this is perfectly fitting for a couple in love that wants to experience the pleasure of orgasm without intercourse.

Becoming a Sexual Guide for Your Partner

Knowing how to pleasure your spouse, of course, is not automatic. Spouses do not come with a manual! A particular type of touch that from your perspective should be pleasurable to your spouse (on the basis of something you saw or read, or that was important in a previous relationship), may in fact feel uncomfortable, even threatening, to her or him. Communication, obviously, becomes a key ingredient in achieving sexual intimacy.

Unless you are willing to offer both verbal and nonverbal clues about your sexual self, your partner is put in an awkward situation. You are your partner's best teacher because no other person knows what excites you like you do. You are the expert on your own sexuality!

BLESSED is the person whose spouse is free to communicate
about sexual needs and desires and explore new horizons.

Obviously, the partner who is receiving information from a spouse that will increase her or his arousal and pleasure needs to hear this as a loving invitation rather than a criticism. Approaching conversation from a "look what I have found out about myself" perspective invites your spouse to participate in something new instead of criticizing her or him for not having knowledge that only you can provide.

If you have any hesitation about talking with your spouse about something you would like to change or experiment with in your sexual encounters, you might find writing a letter to be less threatening. Letters can be carefully crafted, reducing fears of saying the wrong thing. You can add affirmations about what you already enjoy. The spouse can read the letter all the way through without having to respond and will have time to think through your ideas with less defensiveness. Describing what you look forward to can be an invitation to intimacy.

Taking Responsibility for Your Own Satisfaction

Closely related to being your partner's sexual guide is taking responsibility for your own satisfaction. We often see couples in which one partner is blaming the other for an unsatisfying sexual relationship, when in fact they are not willing to communicate what they need and want, or are unwilling to learn about and activate their own arousal patterns. If you are leaving responsibility for your sexual satisfaction with your spouse, then that places an unfair burden on her or him. For your partner to guess what you want and need, much less how you would like to receive it, is next to impossible. In this sense it is imperative for each spouse to accept responsibility for personal sexual fulfillment.

Accepting Your Uniqueness as a Couple

Believing that there is some "normal" sexual activity profile for married people can be a trouble spot if these perceptions become performance goals. Yes, you can read about averages and norms, but they don't come close to describing the wide variety of satisfying patterns. Sexual intimacy is tied to the special desires and expressions of sexuality unique to you and your partner—whatever your chosen frequency and your favorite expressions of sexuality. You and your spouse have the freedom to express your sexual relationship on the basis of what you enjoy and feel comfortable with.

THE MANY MEANINGS
OF SEXUAL ENCOUNTERS

Beyond the basic need for physical satisfaction, sexual encounters meet many other needs such as security, affirmation, and affection.

Couples who identify the various meanings of sexual encounters can be more intentional in communicating what they need and how they need it. Furthermore, recognizing the variety of needs that can be met through a sexual encounter expands a partner's interest in initiating and responding to opportunities because of what these encounters contribute to marital intimacy.

EXERCISE: The Many Meanings of Sexual Encounters

This exercise will help you identify the various meanings which a sexual encounter can have for you and your partner. Take a few minutes and fill it out. Directions are self-explanatory. There is a copy for both you and your partner.

After you finish the exercise take time to discuss what you learned. Using the skills you developed reading the communication chapter, reach a shared meaning about each of the phrases you marked for both yourself and your mate.

Moods differ depending on what else is happening in life, but sexual encounters can be meaningful regardless of mood. Various moods call for sexual encounters with differing nuances, initiatives, and energy levels.

When Andy is feeling "down" about some real or imagined failure to measure up to his ideal self, he likes a sexual encounter to be initiated by Judy. He likes the encounter to be slow, quiet, and gentle. When he is in a celebrative mood he likes to initiate, and is glad if the encounter can be active and playful.

Take the time to understand these various meanings so you can guide your partner in being the best possible lover in any particular situation. Communication about our needs and wants concerning a sexual encounter can include information beyond the physical actions that contribute to our sexual pleasure.

RECOVERING THE PASSION

How can a couple recapture the passion? Most books focus on the physical—learning more about erogenous zones or changing techniques. But more basic to passion is nurturing the erotic potential in each partner and in the relationship. Sexual encounters can certainly be en-

The Many Meanings of Sexual Encounters

Sexual encounters can meet many needs beyond the need for physical satisfaction. We have listed below some of the emotional and rational needs that can be fulfilled through a meaningful sexual encounter. Read the list carefully. Add any phrases which express the unique meanings that sexual encounters have for you or your spouse in the blank spaces at the bottom.

Now choose five of these needs which are frequently most important for you to have met in a sexual encounter with your spouse. Mark them in the first column on the right.

My sexual relationship with you often meets my need for:	Needs which are most important to me	Needs which are most important to my spouse
totally feeling "at one" with you		
affection and touch		
acceptance of my physical/sexual self		
procreation, sharing parenting		
being number one to you		
giving you physical pleasure		
playtime, fun, excitement		
being needed by you		
affirmation of your love		
a deep sense of emotional intimacy		
celebrating our relationship		
security about belonging fully to you		
confirmation of my sexual identity as man/woman		
support, understanding, and caring when life is frustrating		
being treated gently and tenderly		
being sexually attractive to you		

Then choose the five needs which you feel are most important for your spouse to have met in a sexual encounter. Mark these in the second column on the right.

The Many Meanings of Sexual Encounters

Sexual encounters can meet many needs beyond the need for physical satisfaction. We have listed below some of the emotional and rational needs that can be fulfilled through a meaningful sexual encounter. Read the list carefully. Add any phrases which express the unique meanings that sexual encounters have for you or your spouse in the blank spaces at the bottom.

Now choose five of these needs which are frequently most important for you to have met in a sexual encounter with your spouse. Mark them in the first column on the right.

My sexual relationship with you often meets my need for:	Needs which are most important to me	Needs which are most important to my spouse
totally feeling "at one" with you		
affection and touch		
acceptance of my physical/sexual self		
procreation, sharing parenting		
being number one to you		
giving you physical pleasure		
playtime, fun, excitement		
being needed by you		
affirmation of your love		
a deep sense of emotional intimacy		
celebrating our relationship		
security about belonging fully to you		
confirmation of my sexual identity as man/woman		
support, understanding, and caring when life is frustrating		
being treated gently and tenderly		
being sexually attractive to you		

Then choose the five needs which you feel are most important for your spouse to have met in a sexual encounter. Mark these in the second column on the right.

livened by knowledge of the physical aspects of arousal, but attending to the mental process of sexual desire will create the most change. A couple's assessment of "good sex" is related to the intensity of erotic excitement and arousal more than to the physical process.

Sexual desire is certainly rooted in our physical nature, but just "doing it" is not ultimately satisfying to mature persons seeking marital intimacy. Routinely "having sex" is not much more than "mating" in the animal world—necessary for procreation and sexual release, but hardly approaching the "one flesh" potential of human sexuality. "Having sex" is OK, but *making love* is the essence of human sexuality as a sacred experience.

We all have the innate capacity for sexual arousal, but the erotic desire that excites us toward wanting a romantic, passionate sexual experience with our partner must be created. Sexual arousal may take place anytime in response to anyone, but romantic desire has to be created. If partners are having sex simply to satisfy sexual urges then sex quickly becomes routine. Compared with the possibility of passionate sex that they are being reminded of by TV, movies, and magazines, simply "having sex" seems quite boring. The sense of disappointment and deprivation makes both partners vulnerable to erotic opportunities outside of the relationship.

The key to recovery of passion, therefore, is primarily in your mind and heart, not in the body. The most basic aspect of our sexuality is located in our mind. This is where arousal and stimulation occur. Somewhere we have heard it said, "If you are dead in the head you are dead in the bed."

The imagination is a powerful source for discovering our erotic potential. What is erotic for you is particular to your sexual development and imagination. Reading romantic novels or magazine stories, listening to certain kinds of music, watching certain programs on TV, wearing certain clothing (or seeing your partner in certain clothing), being in a specific place, and eating certain foods can all contribute to your readiness for a sexual encounter. Identify them and be intentional to make them part of your preparation for sexual encounters.

EXERCISE: What Turns You On?

Exploring what arouses your erotic interests can add to your participation in sexual encounters. Make a list of clothes, foods, aromas, movies, touches, sounds, settings, and so forth that push *your* erotic buttons. Work on this list for a few weeks. Communicate to your spouse what you learn and describe those actions which she or he can take to arouse you.

Your sexual fantasies offer a good clue about what turns you on. All of us have sexual fantasies, though sometimes we may be embarrassed to identify them. However, from both your night dreams and your day-dreams you can identify those things that excite you about sexuality and those things that frighten or inhibit you. Are you ready to search more carefully for what excites you? The following exercise might be helpful.

EXERCISE: Remembering a Romantic Event
Remember a meaningful, erotic sexual encounter. Now capture what contributed to that experience so that you can learn more about your own erotic keys. Where were you? What was happening? What made it special? What led to your arousal and passion? Add your answers to the list you are making from the previous exercise.

Since you want to create a romantic context for your spouse by attending to those things which arouse and excite her or him, ask your spouse to complete the above exercises. Several other ways to explore your sexual relationship include:

- Read some books together that describe lovemaking and discuss which of the activities you feel comfortable to try.
- Compose a "turn on" list for each partner which states body areas which are particularly sensitive to arousal, activities to which one is particularly responsive, and contextual (music, aroma, clothing, place, and so on) stimulants. Add on to this list over a few months as you discover new areas of self-awareness.
- Take a course from a massage therapist on pleasurable massage which can be shared between partners. Several books also describe how to develop sensual touch.
- Look at some tastefully prepared video tapes which describe and illustrate lovemaking. A marriage therapist can make up-to-date recommendations.

BEHAVIORS THAT MAKE A DIFFERENCE

Being intentional to create an atmosphere for lovemaking communicates to your partner that you find pleasure in the relationship and have an investment in enriching the bonds that keep the marriage dynamic. Actions that stimulate your spouse will invite more arousal. Planning opportunities to experience erotic pleasures is a wonderful way of "making love."

Plan a Romantic Event

Sexuality and sensuality are closely entwined. Being romantic includes the awareness that touching, smelling, seeing, hearing, and tasting are important. The music, the aroma (candles, incense), the material of the clothing, the taste of the food, the warmth of the wine, can all enhance the sensuousness of the occasion.

> After discussing sexuality in a marriage enrichment class we assigned the couples the challenge of thinking through the planning of a romantic event. Darlene and Kent reported several weeks later that they had made a covenant to take turns every week planning a romantic context in which to enjoy a sexual encounter. Darlene chose to plan a "beach party." She got posters from a local travel agency to place around their living room, put blankets on the floor, and put on the bikini he liked best. The preparation was exciting for her and when he came home from the library that Friday night the sparks flew!

Take Risks, Be Unconventional

Routine can be secure, but also boring. Are you having sexual encounters in the same place, at the same time, with the same approach? Recognize that doing something daring, risky, or unconventional can add passion to sexual encounters.

> Erik and Joanna described a sexual encounter that made them feel excited and connected. They left a romantic movie that had aroused Joanna. She teased and kissed Erik all the way home. When they arrived home she increased her initiatives and Erik responded. They slid the passenger seat back and made love right in the garage.

> Lee and Gwen discussed the passion they felt when having sexual encounters in motel rooms when their school-age children were

trying to go to sleep in the other bed. Wanting to enjoy touch, but without movement or noise that would draw attention from the children, challenged both of them to search for physical strategies and positions that were unusual for them and heightened their excitement. They described these experiences as quite passionate and intimate.

Nicholas pointed out that some of the most passionate lovemaking that occurred in the early years of his marriage with Sheila took place in the guest bedroom at her parents' home. She agreed with this assessment and was sure that she was aroused by participating in something that her parents had been so negative about while she was growing up. She felt that she was establishing her new role as an adult, showing her independence, and communicating a level of passion that she suspected was lacking in her parents' relationship.

Affirmation

Each of us desires approval from the person with whom we are in love and involved with romantically. We never lose the need to feel that our sexual self, our basic masculinity and femininity, is attractive to our spouse. We are deeply pleased when our lover finds us attractive, enjoys how we make love, and finds pleasure in sexual encounters with us. Does your spouse know what there is about her or his physical self that you admire and turns you on? Have you told your partner recently how wonderful you find her or his lovemaking skills? Have you described how excited you get in her or his presence? We bet you did when you were courting, and remember what a turn-on it was to hear those wonderful affirmations?

It is not unusual for us to ask a couple in therapy, "What attracted you to each other in the first place?" Often a first response is focused on sexual attraction. "I thought she was gorgeous!" or "He was so good looking!" A second response is often, "She seemed to really be attracted to me." In short, attraction and acceptance of your sexual self is basic to feeling erotic and passionate. You can enhance sexual intimacy immediately by taking time to tell your spouse the specifics about her or him that turn you on, affirming those characteristics and behaviors which you find so attractive.

IT TAKES TWO

Love Letters

One romantic way of expressing affirmation is through love letters. Writing has largely disappeared from courtship rituals, but if you did write letters to one another before marriage you may remember them as special. Why not write a love letter reminding your partner of the aspects of your lovemaking that you particularly enjoy. Perhaps you could offer an invitation to a special sexual encounter, or describe sexual fantasies that he or she would find exciting and inviting.

IF DIFFICULTIES ARISE

We recently opened a small appliance and noted a section called "In Case of Difficulty" that listed things to check if the appliance was not working. If you and your spouse are experiencing particular frustrations and dissatisfactions with your sexual relationship, consider the following issues as possible explanations.

Sexuality and Power

Sexual dissatisfaction is often related to power struggles in the partnership. Using the ideas in chapter 5, evaluate whether or not the relationship has become unequal. Has one partner acted without the consent of the other? Has one of you made a decision about spending money, or where to live, or something else that has left one partner feeling devalued, unimportant, or used? Are decisions about sexual interaction mutual, or have you slipped into patterns that make one partner feel out of control or devalued?

Early Stories about Gender Roles

Each partner enters the relationship with different stories about sexuality. These stories include beliefs that shape our expectations about which gender takes initiative, has the strongest drive, has the most emotional needs, and should take responsibility for sexual fulfillment. Paying attention to these past stories and their effect on us in the present is one way of accepting responsibility for our contribution to sexual intimacy.

Theological Background

You or your partner may have been raised in a context where religious authorities and parents used scripture or tradition to make you afraid of the erotic potential in humans. Instead of learning how to integrate sexuality into your life you may have only learned of its dangers and protected yourself by suppressing your erotic capacities. You may think that exploring your erotic potential is not "right," something that "good" people don't do. Allowing yourself to think sexual thoughts might feel like inviting evil into your life, or sinning, or angering God.

These religious authorities may have put limitations on the types of sexual activities that are "normal" and permissible for a couple, labeling everything else as "perversions." You probably experience some anxiety or inhibition about certain behaviors, such as oral stimulation. If you discover such hesitancy, read more thoroughly about theology and sex so that you can develop your own understanding about God and sexuality. If you imagine God to be frowning or shaking a critical parental finger in your direction when you are being sexual, then you have an image of God that needs transforming. Remember that scripture puts no inhibitions on enjoying each other. Whatever you mutually agree upon as pleasurable, and communicates respect and care, makes God smile.

Unresolved Conflict

When a couple is in the middle of a conflict, or when chronic anger goes unresolved, sexual intimacy is not easy. It is difficult to give to and receive from a spouse with whom we are angry. Chronic resentments make it difficult to give one's self in a sexual encounter. Entering a sexual encounter is more satisfying when conflict has been confronted and resolution accomplished. Use chapter 4 on anger and conflict to address unresolved anger.

Body Image

Negative body image can detract from sexual intimacy. You may be deeply convinced that you are unattractive and could not possibly be the source of arousal and sexual excitation, even to the one you believe loves you. Such a belief makes it difficult to present yourself in the spontaneous, free, unselfconscious manner that marks the most passionate sexual encounters. It is important to take your partner's af-firmation of your sexual self at face value and accept her or his attrac-tion to you, whether or not you are able to feel good about your own physical attributes. Discounting your partner's affirmations frustrates her or him.

If either you or your partner has undergone some major challenge to her or his body image, such as vasectomy, prostectomy, hysterectomy, mastectomy, or amputation, it becomes important to discuss changes in feelings and thoughts. Sexual desire and arousal patterns will prob-ably change for both partners. Seek to affirm those aspects of sexuality that excite you, but also look for new ways to understand and express sexuality between you. A common change in body image for younger couples occurs during and after pregnancy when the wife might feel quite different about her body.

Another issue around body image is physical attractiveness. You might ask what responsibility you are taking for your physical attrac-tiveness. Are you maintaining the physical shape and size (within the limitations of health and age) that your spouse enjoys? Are you pre-senting yourself physically (washing, shaving, clipping toenails) in ways that are sensuous to your spouse rather than turn-offs?

Sex Education

We have not dealt with the "plumbing" aspects of sexual encoun-ters, assuming that the reader knows this information. However, you may have had inadequate sex education, either formal or informal. Learning more about the physiology of sex could enhance your ability as a sexual partner. Numerous books provide information and exer-cises that will help you know more completely your own physiology and that of your partner. Furthermore, sex education, whether formal or informal, does not usually deal adequately with the emotional, rela-tional, affectional, and spiritual aspects of sexuality. You might find it helpful to learn more about the psychology of sexuality (see "For Fur-ther Reading" at the end of this chapter).

Problems in Sexual Functioning

Sexual fulfillment is more difficult when a couple faces functional difficulties, such as premature ejaculation, impotence, inhibited sexual desire, or pain during intercourse. Some difficulties in sexual function occur because of chronic diseases, as the side effect of medication, or as a result of some particular physical condition. Medical information and intervention is available. Waiting will not help and sexual intimacy may take a nosedive. See your doctor.

Ghosts from the Past

Unresolved emotional conflicts such as fear, anxiety, guilt, shame, or mistrust can also inhibit sexual fulfillment. You may read about spontaneous, passionate sexual interactions in this chapter with a tinge of despair because you find it difficult to participate with freedom in any sexual encounter. You feel tense, inhibited, and duty bound rather than joyfully excited. Your next step would be to search for those factors inhibiting your full participation in sexual intimacy.

Past stories from previous sexual experiences, significant other partners, and the family in which we grew up, can make positive or negative contributions to our sexual experience. Pay close attention to any experience that diminishes your ability to give and receive in sexual encounters. Your next step in dealing with emotional barriers to enjoying sexual encounters may be finding therapeutic help. A competent professional can help you sort through these past stories and regain the freedom for sexual pleasure which God has made possible.

BLESSED is the spouse whose partner goes the second mile
in overcoming barriers to sexual fulfillment.

FOR FURTHER READING

Nelson, James B. *Embodiment: An Approach to Sexuality and Christian Theology*. Minneapolis: Augsburg Publishing House, 1978.

Penner, Clifford, and Joyce Penner. *The Gift of Sex: A Christian Guide to Sexual Fulfillment*. Waco, Tex.: Word Books, 1981.

———. *Men and Sex: Discovering Greater Love, Passion, and Intimacy with Your Wife*. Nashville, Tenn.: Thomas Nelson, Inc., 1997.

———. *Restoring the Pleasure*. Dallas: Word Publishing, 1993.

Rey, Caroline, ed. *The Mammoth Book of Love and Sensuality*. New York: Carroll and Graf Publishers, 1997.

seven

SHARING THE SPIRITUAL JOURNEY
Forgiveness and Justice

Our wedding took place at our local church in the context of worship. We were convinced of God's blessing on our relationship. Like many of you, we were assuming that our marriage would be shaped by our Christian faith, but with little understanding of what that might mean. We knew we would be active members of a church, participating together in worship and service, and probably praying together at mealtime, but beyond that the possibilities for sharing a spiritual pilgrimage were vague. We learned that practicing spirituality as a couple is not easy and must be pursued intentionally. As the years passed we found ways to join each other's faith journey. We became aware of many specific practices that contribute significantly to the meaningfulness of our relationship and the overall sense of intimacy.

MARRIAGE: A CONTEXT
FOR SPIRITUAL REVELATION

One reason we consider marriage a gift from God is because of its potential for revealing deeper spiritual truths. The love shared between husband and wife can reveal deeper meanings about God's love for us. Marriage can be like a window through which we see more clearly how love expresses itself in trust, acceptance, and forgiveness. Likewise, our encounters with God prepare us for deeper encounters with our spouse. In this way our spiritual growth enhances our marriage, and nurturing our marriage gives us insight about our spiritual lives.

Many partners have found that their marriage relationship opened up possibilities for spiritual development. Some people learn to trust a spouse more than they have ever trusted another human and from that experience learn to trust God at deeper levels. Others have experienced in marriage a level of acceptance and depth of care unlike anything in their personal history, enabling them to "hear" the gospel's claim that God loves us unconditionally and cares for us deeply.

> Keoni grew up in a family that practiced no religious tradition. His family was critical and abusive, particularly of him, the last of three sons. His father was an alcoholic and emotionally abusive and his mentally ill mother was physically abusive. The result was a terrible sense of unworthiness and shame. He met Rose as a senior in high school. She and her family were deeply religious people and accepted Keoni unconditionally. They took him to church and taught him the Christian faith as understood in their tradition. They believed that God loved all people and that grace was available to all. Keoni and Rose married one year after graduating from high school. Rose challenged his low self-regard by her mature love and affection. As an adult Keoni credits her constant love and acceptance with his growing experience of God's love and acceptance.

Acceptance by a spouse who accepts our idiosyncrasies and loves us anyway, in spite of what he or she knows about us, is an experience of God's grace. As we said in the last chapter, many couples have experienced within the merging of selves during sexual encounters a deeper understanding of the ecstatic connection possible in mystical experiences, worship, and private devotion.

RESPONSIBILITY FOR
YOUR SPIRITUAL PILGRIMAGE

A basic reality about spirituality in marriage is that each partner must take primary responsibility for her or his own spiritual pilgrimage. Your partner can contribute to your spiritual growth, but the final accountability is with you. We cannot depend on the marital relationship to provide all of the content and the nurture necessary for spiritual development. A marriage can be an extension of the "family of God," but cannot take the place of the community of faith (the church) and private spiritual disciplines.

Some people find that involvement in courtship and the beginnings of a marital relationship seems to lead them away from personal practice of spiritual disciplines. The excitement of this wonderful new relationship, the number of tasks involved in setting up a home, the establishment of a new social life, and the differences in religious practice (to which we will return later) can reduce the time and energy invested in spiritual life.

If you practiced spiritual disciplines prior to marriage, then continuing them in marriage is important. You know what circumstances and activities are more likely to make it possible for you, in all your uniqueness, to sense the presence of God (reading books, listening to certain music, writing poetry, meditating, visiting places that have become sacred to you, singing songs, praying, keeping a journal, appreciating art, reflecting on scripture). Are you taking the time and expending the energy to practice those disciplines that set the context for a possible encounter with God?

A spouse who is attending to her or his own spiritual development is also making a contribution to marital growth. Spiritual experiences that deepen our spiritual awareness expand our perception of the potential for marital intimacy. As we become more aware of our connections with the rest of creation and with the Creator, we understand more about the potential for intimacy with our spouse.

PRACTICING FAITH
TOWARD OUR SPOUSE

An obvious way to allow faith to inform and shape our marriage is by expressing our faith within the relationship—that is, loving our partner by practicing Christian attitudes and behaviors. Whatever your tradition, you have been taught that believers are committed to live in a manner that reflects that our lives have been transformed by our encounters with the gospel and our commitment to the living God. Below are some ideas from the Christian tradition that can inform practicing our faith toward our spouse.

Priests to One Another

Many Christian traditions share a belief in the "priesthood of believers." This doctrine proclaims that every believer is called to be a witness to, and a mediator of, God's grace. All Christians are to minister to others in a manner that expresses God's love. Notice the egalitarian nature of this doctrine. Both male and female, husband and wife, are called to represent Christ to others.

Now consider that your spouse is also a brother or sister in the faith, a person created in God's image and for whom Christ died. You have the privilege and responsibility to function as a priest to her or him. We are an extension of the incarnation, witnesses in the flesh to the Word of God. You are encouraged and challenged by this priesthood of believers doctrine to be a channel of grace to your spouse.

Love Your Neighbor as Yourself

When Jesus was asked, "What is the greatest commandment?" he did not answer indirectly, nor dodge the significance of the question. He answered clearly and concisely,

> The first is, "Hear, O Israel: the Lord our God, the Lord is one; you shall love the Lord your God with all your heart, and with all your soul, and with all your mind, and with all your strength." The second is this, "You shall love your neighbor as yourself." There is no other commandment greater than these. (Mark 12:29–31)

Loving your neighbor as yourself is not a new idea to you, but perhaps you had not thought of your spouse as a neighbor. If we are to love our neighbors as ourselves, would it not make sense that we would love our spouse even more? Perhaps this is what the writer of Ephesians has in mind when challenging husbands to love their wives: "Husbands should love their wives as they do their own bodies. He who loves his wife loves himself" (Eph. 5:28). Later, this same author says that a husband "should love his wife as himself" (Eph. 5:33).

Practicing "The Fruit of the Spirit"

The early Christians believed that the transforming love of the risen Christ had given them this responsibility to love their neighbors as they loved themselves. The apostle Paul wrote about this in several of his letters, offering specific descriptions of how life in the Spirit might look as practiced in relationships. In Galatians, Paul describes these characteristics of Christian living as fruit of the Spirit: "love, joy, peace, patience, kindness, generosity, faithfulness, gentleness, and self-control" (Gal. 5:22–24). We find that these characteristics are important contributors to an intimate marriage. Couples who use these in assessing their relationship have found help in knowing how to deepen intimacy.

EXERCISE: How Are the Fruits of the Spirit
                Present in Your Marriage?
   On the next page is an exercise that will allow you to make such an assessment. You will see a list of the fruits of the Spirit with the possible meanings expanded by other concepts.

1.   Take a moment to read the instructions and then complete the exercise. When you finish, return to this section.
2.   What did you learn from this exercise? Compare your sheet with your partner's. You will probably find areas within the relationship that could use some attention.
3.   Ask your partner for help in identifying specific behaviors that would allow you to develop the fruits which are either barely present or moderately at work in the relationship.
4.   Using the covenant-making process from chapter 8, work toward specific agreements that provide opportunity for growth.

NURTURING SPIRITUAL INTIMACY

   As you pursue your own spiritual pilgrimage you can find meaningful ways to share this pilgrimage with your spouse. Along the way, you may learn ways to support and encourage your partner to take the time to experience the presence of God and affirm her or his spiritual pilgrimage. To promote spiritual intimacy calls for finding ways in which the two of you can nurture a shared journey of faith.

Sharing Sacred Stories

   Each partner has a sacred story, a faith developed over the years that provides an understanding of God, faith, church, prayer, and ethics.

"Fruit of the Spirit" Exercise

In Galatians 5, Paul proclaims that in Jesus Christ we have been set free to "love your neighbor as yourself" (v.14). Paul specifies what this loving is about when he describes the fruit of the spirit (vv. 22–24). Listed below are the fruits Paul mentions, plus some words which elaborate on their meaning.

Put an "X" in the right-hand column to evaluate how much each fruit is present in the ways you relate to your spouse. Now go back and mark with a "Y" to indicate how much you feel each fruit is present in the way your spouse relates to you.

	Barely Present		Present		Strongly Present
Fruit of the Spirit	1	2	3	4	5
Love (compassionate, caring, self-giving, forgiving, intimate, affectionate)					
Joy (spontaneous, celebrative, happy, ecstatic, fun, playful, thankful)					
Peace (calm, content, reassuring, trusting, serene)					
Patience (long-suffering, tolerant, accepting, understanding, hopeful)					
Kindness (thoughtful, courteous, considerate, respectful, empathic)					
Generosity (gracious, generous, giving, sharing, helpful)					
Faithfulness (dependable, trustworthy, committed, loyal)					
Gentleness (tender, sensitive, careful, warm, easy)					
Self-Control (intentional, disciplined, responsible)					

Circle the one that you could commit yourself to work on this next week.

"Fruit of the Spirit" Exercise

In Galatians 5, Paul proclaims that in Jesus Christ we have been set free to "love your neighbor as yourself" (v.14). Paul specifies what this loving is about when he describes the fruit of the spirit (vv. 22–24). Listed below are the fruits Paul mentions, plus some words which elaborate on their meaning.

Put an "X" in the right-hand column to evaluate how much each fruit is present in the ways you relate to your spouse. Now go back and mark with a "Y" to indicate how much you feel each fruit is present in the way your spouse relates to you.

Fruit of the Spirit	Barely Present 1	2	Present 3	4	Strongly Present 5
Love (compassionate, caring, self-giving, forgiving, intimate, affectionate)					
Joy (spontaneous, celebrative, happy, ecstatic, fun, playful, thankful)					
Peace (calm, content, reassuring, trusting, serene)					
Patience (long-suffering, tolerant, accepting, understanding, hopeful)					
Kindness (thoughtful, courteous, considerate, respectful, empathic)					
Generosity (gracious, generous, giving, sharing, helpful)					
Faithfulness (dependable, trustworthy, committed, loyal)					
Gentleness (tender, sensitive, careful, warm, easy)					
Self-Control (intentional, disciplined, responsible)					

Circle the one that you could commit yourself to work on this next week.

Sacred stories often include particular religious events or spiritual experiences which have made a significant contribution to the shape of a partner's faith, even transforming her or his life. These spiritual experiences may have a strong mystical component and by their very nature are almost unspeakable. That is, they are almost beyond words, difficult to describe because it seems impossible to capture them with our normal vocabulary.

These significant experiences have a sacred quality which makes us feel protective of them. Though basic to a person's faith and identity, they are usually private and often go unspoken. They must be handled with care and entrusted only to those we know will treat them as sacred. In a culture that does not know how to respond to experiences that may seem irrational and intensely emotional, sharing these stories is not easy.

> BLESSED is the spouse whose partner will share
> thoughts and feelings about spiritual matters.

We find that spirituality is one of the most difficult topics for couples to discuss. We have asked individuals in marriage enrichment events to remember a formative spiritual experience (a time when they sensed the presence of God, responded to a calling, received a blessing, experienced a vision, or made a vow) which contributed to their spiritual identity and commitments. Then we ask if they have shared the story with their spouse. It is surprising how many have never attempted to communicate these meaningful religious experiences with their partner. Needless to say, those couples who choose to share their sacred stories know each other at a deeper level and share intimacy of a more profound kind.

EXERCISE: Share a Sacred Story
Identify several special events in life which you felt were spiritual in nature and gave shape to your faith. You may call these occurrences by different names: mystical experience, conversion, divine/human encounter, vision, or with some other phrase. But whatever your tradition leads you to call these happenings (or you can leave them nameless), try to put some words together that describe them.

Then, during quiet times together, share these stories with your spouse. Invite your spouse to do the same.

Practicing Spirituality Together

Couples who want to share a spiritual pilgrimage can be intentional in searching for ways to nurture such a bond. The following activities have contributed to the sense of spiritual intimacy for many couples.

- Celebrating special seasons of the Christian year, particularly Advent, Christmas, Lent, and Easter.

  > During each Lenten season, the Tolberts discuss, and then decide upon, a new discipline they can share as a couple. They make a covenant to guide them in expressing this new discipline. Two years ago they gave up watching TV during Lent and committed to read two books about spiritual growth and development instead. During this past Lenten season they decided to fast for twenty-four hours from after breakfast on Saturday until breakfast on Sunday for four weeks. They are quick to describe how these covenants help them feel united in their spiritual pilgrimage.

- Taking spiritual retreats together can include opportunities for each partner to practice spiritual disciplines that are personally meaningful (music, reading, prayer, meditation, writing, scripture). This private time can be balanced with time together in which you share in spiritual disciplines that create a sense of communion with each other and with God.

  > The Giffords chose to rent a cabin in the mountains for a Friday night through Sunday afternoon retreat. Their two girls stayed with grandparents so that they could be alone for this retreat. They decided in advance to spend Friday night and Saturday morning walking, reading, and talking. Then from Saturday noon until Sunday noon they decided to do the same activities but in complete silence. They were fascinated at the nonverbal communication that developed between them as they prepared meals and initiated walks. Most surprising was an unexpected sexual encounter that occurred without any words. They

were excited by the new dimensions of arousal that they experienced. They enjoyed a deeper level of intimacy in their marriage for months afterward, particularly in expressions of their Christian commitments.

- Reading books about faith and theology, both fiction and nonfiction, and discussing your responses.

    Teresa and Juan read religious biographies to each other when traveling, or before going to bed, and then share the contributions to their spiritual pilgrimage. They consciously choose characteristics of these spiritual giants that they would like to incorporate into their own lives and then plan specific ways that this can be accomplished.

- Developing shared rituals that provide a sense of intentionality about inviting God's presence, such as reading religious poetry, singing hymns, or prayer at mealtime or bedtime.

    Reggie and Shanise love music. He sings in a quartet, she in an ensemble, and both sing in the church choir. Most nights before they go to bed they sing a religious song together as their expression of devotion.

- Participating in a "cause" through which you express your commitment to justice.

    The Stevensons colead the AIDS care team in their congregation.

    Henry and Nadine provide brief foster care for preschoolers whose parents are in crisis.

    The Lawrences are heavily involved in education reform.

- Working in a conjoint ministry within a local congregation.

    We often team-teach a church school class, which gives us a structured opportunity to discuss faith issues related to the subjects we are teaching.

- Calling together like-minded couples who are interested in meeting on a regular basis to pursue spiritual development through reading, meditation, instruction, discussion, and so forth.

  > At a local church a group of ten couples meets once a month to discuss marriage. They have been doing this for over five years and know each other well. They are particularly interested in exploring how their faith influences the marital relationship.

- Reading, studying, and reflecting on Bible stories.

  > The Robinsons made a covenant for one year to spend thirty minutes every Wednesday evening reading and studying the Bible. They chose a layperson's commentary. They took turns reading the scripture verses and the commentary to one another. Then they engaged in conversation about what they could learn about their theology and their practice of faith, both within their own relationship and in the larger world.

- Listening to music which is meaningful to both as a source of spiritual reflection and worship.

You might experiment with several of these activities that fit your particular partnership, depending on points of view, levels of comfort, personality differences, and religious experience. If you have children, they can be involved in many of these processes—a wonderful way to pass on the faith.

BARRIERS TO A SHARED JOURNEY

Experiencing spiritual intimacy is no easy task. Many couples come from different religious backgrounds. Even those who grew up in the same faith tradition find that their different personalities and varied spiritual experiences make sharing a spiritual journey difficult. Often partners view spiritual matters through diverse lenses. Let's examine these barriers more closely.

Conflicting Religious Traditions

Religious language, doctrine, forms of worship, religious ritual, the practice of spiritual disciplines, religious authority, and theology vary among faith traditions. Even couples from the same faith tradition may experience significant differences between "low" and "high" forms of worship, differing views on the understanding of scripture, and conservative and liberal perspectives on theology and ethics. Contrasting understandings of how God works in the world, for example, can challenge spiritual intimacy.

> Theological differences were identified by Roger and Gwen as causing conflict and interfering with their sense of intimacy. Roger's sense of God focused on transcendence. God seemed more holy and what Roger called "beyond us," so he had little faith that God was "pulling the strings" behind life's day-to-day happenings. Gwen's concept of God emphasized immanence and she had a deep sense of God's "guiding hand" informing and leading her through life. Roger was uncomfortable when Gwen would ask him to pray with her about a decision they needed to make. When he resisted she felt that he was withdrawing from "spiritual closeness." They chose to learn more about each other's spiritual journey and religious perspectives. They worked at accepting and respecting their different viewpoints. Then they intentionally found those aspects of their faith that they shared and focused on those similarities for sharing spiritual intimacy.

Personality Differences

Along with one's religious tradition, personality differences significantly influence the manner in which each partner pursues the spiritual journey, particularly with reference to worship.

> Dan and Martha were both divorced and seeking premarital counseling before entering into their second marriage. A central issue was their desire to make this marriage more clearly informed by their religious faith. They wanted to embark on a shared spiritual journey. Their difficulty was in finding a local congregation where they could both find meaning in worship. Their personalities and religious traditions were quite different, which affected the type of worship they

found meaningful. The "places" in which they felt the presence of God were totally opposite. Dan was most at home with what he called "the majesty of God," Martha with the "friendship that Jesus offered the disciples." Dan was introverted and preferred a large church where he could go unnoticed. He liked the anonymity and the ritualized liturgy of the Episcopal cathedral. Martha was extroverted and enjoyed the warmth and "know everyone" feel of a small congregation. She preferred the folksy and informal structure of her small Methodist fellowship. He could not sense God's presence in this "coffee shop mentality," as he called it. She, on the other hand, felt cold, alone, and distant from God in what she called the "moldy cave" of the cathedral. They worked to accept their differences and to learn to support the other's spiritual needs. They made a covenant to attend early services at his church and the 11:00 A.M. service at her church. Slowly they began to appreciate the strength of each one's tradition. Most important, they felt support from each other for their faith journey.

Persons with different personalities relate to God differently. Spiritual exercises and disciplines that are most meaningful to one person may not be to another. The section on personality differences in chapter 2 might offer further clues to explain your unique responses to spiritual issues.

Embarrassment

Embarrassment about one's childlike faith, religious doubts, or theological ignorance also can hinder sharing one's spiritual pilgrimage. If one partner is perceived to be more religious, or more educated in spiritual things, then the other spouse may feel vulnerable.

Elston was a computer programmer when his wife, Chelsea, who had always worked in the church, went to divinity school at a nearby university. He was fascinated by her books and read several of her papers, but understood little of this academic work. Her conversations with fellow students with whom she studied were beyond his comprehension. His faith was important to him, but it was a "feeling thing," he said, and not something he felt comfortable trying to put into words. He and Chelsea finally decided that sharing their spiritual pilgrimage could best take place in the practical expression of their faith, rather than in philosophical discussions. She met that need with her fellow students. She and Elston became involved in their church's ministry to the homeless, which gave them a mutually satisfying way of sharing their faith.

Guilt about the distance between our spiritual ideals and the realities of our own faults and weaknesses may make a spouse feel awkward about discussing spiritual issues. We may feel ashamed when sharing faith with a spouse who knows only too well the gap between what we "preach" and what we "practice."

Allen is twenty-seven years old and recently married. He grew up in a Christian home, but one where he experienced significant hostility between his parents. He had high hopes for his ability to bring his Christian ideals into his marriage with Pam. He had not expected to express his "mom's temper" so intensely and inappropriately at Pam. They had both been shocked by his anger. Allen was disillusioned in himself and was ashamed to even represent himself as a Christian to Pam. One evening in a marriage enrichment retreat he declared, "I thought I was a pretty decent Christian until I got married, but now I am more like a pagan in the way I treat Pam. I know she wonders why I even go to church." He went on to say that his embarrassment and guilt made him unwilling to discuss religious matters with Pam. He was willing to make an appointment with a pastoral counselor to assess the anger and to explore what his faith taught about acceptance and forgiveness.

Gender and Spirituality

As stated in earlier chapters, we only know ourselves, others, and the world around us through our engendered self. Our identity is shaped in definitive ways by being male or female. It should be obvious that our understanding of God, the meaning of our divine/human encounters, and the processes by which we worship and practice our faith are influenced by our maleness and femaleness. It is not realistic to think that our spirituality is somehow neutered and unrelated to our sexuality. To deepen their spirituality, for example, men can overcome their socialized tendency to inhibit their emotions and to be suspicious of mutual intimacy, both of which can keep their relationship with God at a distance. Women, on the other hand, may be inhibited in their relationship with God if they lack a clearly defined sense of self.

Given their different perspectives of God, what it means to encounter God, and of spirituality in general, husbands and wives can share their unique spiritual experience so that each partner's awareness of God can be expanded. The different perspectives of each partner's spiritual pilgrimage can be enhanced by sharing and learning about the spirituality of the other. Traditional traits assigned to male and female may lead to different expressions of faith.

> Since they met and married in college during the '70s, Lucy and Gilbert have been working against injustice, but in significantly different ways. Gilbert is strongly characterized by traits identified in our culture as masculine. He is assertive, even aggressive, and does not mind "in your face" confrontations. His work against injustice is expressed "on the streets," as he calls it, through organized protests, visiting city council meetings, and writing open letters to the editor. Lucy is quiet and dislikes confrontation. Her work against injustice is focused on what she calls "peacemaking." To foster deeper understanding and compassion, she plans events that bring persons of differing lifestyles and experiences together with hope that deeper understanding will foster peace and justice. For example, she orchestrates luncheon meetings at which "straight" church members dialogue with gays and lesbians. Lucy and Gilbert fully support each other's expressions of ministry and neither expects the other to do it "my way."

Alienation

Another barrier to sharing the spiritual journey is when partners become estranged. Alienation with each other makes it unlikely that we can with any sincerity share spiritual concerns. The anger, sadness, and loneliness generated by this experience of separation leaves us out of communion. Partners who want to regain a sense of togetherness on their spiritual pilgrimage must bridge this alienation.

> BLESSED is the spouse whose partner seeks to overcome
> the barriers to sharing the spiritual journey.

Overcoming this alienation is so important to spiritual intimacy that we will focus next on forgiveness and reconciliation.

REPENTANCE, CONFESSION, FORGIVENESS, AND RECONCILIATION

Given the intimacy of our marital relationships, we have the power to hurt each other more deeply than can persons outside the relationship. We have made ourselves vulnerable because our partners know us more thoroughly than most other persons. They know our weaknesses and our sensitive areas, making it possible to shoot arrows of ridicule, accusation, unfaithfulness, or uncaring into the heart of our vulnerability. We are tempted to respond in kind because of our hurt and anger. The wounds caused by these arrows create alienation and block intimacy. Only repentance, confession, and forgiveness can break the cycle of anger, blame, and pain—and open the way for healing and reconciliation. If confession and repentance are not offered, bitterness and resentment fester and become the cancerous cells that can kill a marriage.

Empathy and Reconciliation

Forgiveness is not easy because our disillusionment, anger, hurt, and resentment can run deep. Forgiveness can only occur when empathy allows each partner to step into the other's shoes and understand her or his view of the situation. This empathy is a two-way street. The wound*ing* partner works at understanding the sense of woundedness. The wound*ed* partner works at understanding how the transgressor's personal story and personality led to the unloving word, attitude, or behavior. Knowing and being known are crucial in allowing each partner to identify with the other, and to express informed confession and repentance on the one hand and forgiveness on the other.

Confession and Repentance

When our actions hurt our spouse and cause estrangement, then our faith calls us to repent and confess. Repentance is the act of accepting responsibility for wounding our spouse. Confession is the process of communicating by word and behavior that we are indeed sorry for the wounding. Restitution is the act of restoration, when possible. Repentance, confession, and restitution combined are an act of love, as is the forgiveness extended by the wounded partner.

Repentance and confession can begin constructing the bridge of re-connection after word or deed has caused estrangement. They are the spiritual initiatives that can heal wounds. They set the stage for putting aside resentment, resolving the hurt, beginning the healing process, and restoring your sense of intimacy. How? Genuine confession and repentance invite forgiveness from your spouse.

The marriage between Colette and Douglas was stable, but Colette came to a pastoral counselor because of current anger that was inter-fering with their relationship. She was pregnant, the result of an un-planned, unprotected sexual encounter.

Douglas often traveled out of town on company business for days at a time. On a recent weekend she had joined him for a "getaway" weekend. Their first night together was romantic and both were highly aroused. When moving toward intercourse, they realized that no condoms were available. She knew that she was in a vulnerable time in her menstrual cycle and wanted to stop the proceedings. Douglas pushed for consummation, arguing that pregnancy was a long shot. Against her better judgment she "sort of" consented, but basically "gave in" because "he was so insistent."

Now she was pregnant. They had three teenage boys and Colette had returned to her career nine years ago. She had no interest in rais-ing another child and was faced with the difficult decision of whether to have the child or abort the pregnancy. She was intensely angry at Douglas for "demanding" intercourse. He felt attacked and defen-sive, wanting her to share responsibility for the pregnancy, which left her feeling hurt, victimized, devalued, and isolated.

Only when he was able to confess that he knew he had pushed against her wishes and expressed his remorse about his use of power, did her anger diminish. His expression of concern about the result-ing pregnancy, and the hard decision that was now in front of them, invited her to move from feeling isolated to feeling some together-ness in their life situation.

The Gift of Forgiveness

The gift of forgiveness toward a spouse reflects our appreciation for the mercy and forgiveness which comes to us through the grace of God's love. Forgiveness restores the relationship between us and God, and has the capacity to restore marital communion. Since forgiveness is one of the major ways in which God has expressed love toward us, we can model this love through forgiveness offered to a spouse. Forgiveness overcomes the alienation and creates the impetus toward going forward into new depths of intimacy.

Change in Behavior

Confession and repentance must be followed by changes in behavior. Though our faith calls us to forgive often, it does not demand that we live continuously with destructive behavior. After all, if confession and repentance have occurred, the transgressing spouse will want to change behavior as a move toward restoration, and the wounded partner will expect the transgressing spouse to continue this commitment to change. The couple can be intentional about this change by using the exercises in chapter 8 to identify needs and make covenants that lead in different directions.

Cheap Forgiveness

Some Christians are taught that forgiveness must be automatic and quick. Often this cheap forgiveness is given in order to halt the conflict. They respond more out of fear that more destruction will take place. At other times cheap forgiveness is offered by someone whose sense of self is not strong enough to feel deserving of a change in the spouse's behavior. Ultimately, however, cheap forgiveness leaves the wound unattended, the wounding partner without an opportunity to grow, and the relationship less intimate because no lasting change in behavior has occurred.

Forgiving and Not Forgetting

Contrary to a popular concept, forgiving does not mean forgetting, at least not in the sense of blotting out our memory of the transgression. We will be wise to practice what Lewis Smedes calls "redemptive remembering" in *Forgive and Forget*. To remember is to take the wounding seriously. Remembering is redemptive because it allows each partner to keep conscious the lessons learned, which can prevent another occurrence. The wound*ing* partner must remember in order to change behavior. The wound*ed* partner must remember in order to know where to draw the boundaries next time and how not to be overly vulnerable too soon. To remember gives us an opportunity to learn about ourselves and our temptations and protects us from repeating the offense. To remember gives us content for our covenants and motivation for achieving deeper intimacy.

If remembering is to be redemptive, however, we will not allow it to be the lens through which we view every future interaction. We will not consider the transgression as ammunition for the next battle, or the guillotine over our partner's neck. Rather, we will slowly reestablish trust and make ourselves vulnerable again. Sins against each other leave scars even after the wounds heal. But these scars can be symbols of our resilience and reminders of what can be redeemed in relationships when we accept our limitations and forgive our sins.

To continue focusing on the wound, keeping it front and center in your heart and mind, is to live in the past. The relationship is shackled to the past and, therefore, to hopelessness. Forgiveness, on the other hand, is a dynamic which looks to the future and allows the creation of new future stories which nurture hope.

LOVE CALLS US TO JUSTICE

You may be surprised to find the word "justice" in a book on marriage, but Christian faith calls for us to be concerned about justice in every relationship. Micah, the Hebrew prophet, chastises his congregation for thinking they could please God through worship, even though they were not living righteously. He reminds them that God's real desire has been clearly revealed, "He has told you, O mortal, what is good; and what does the Lord require of you but to do justice, and to love kindness, and to walk humbly with your God?" (6:8). Applied to married couples, we can say that God is not pleased unless our ways of relating to one another are characterized by justice and righteousness and marked by kindness and humility.

Our society frequently thinks of justice in terms of finding out who is right and wrong and punishing people for wrongdoing. The concept of justice in scripture has a different connotation, because it refers to God's concern for the rights of all persons to be treated with respect and to have their basic needs met by the community. This is the heart of God's expectation as addressed through the prophet Amos, who reminds us in 5:21–24 of what God really requires. Verse 24 says, "Let justice roll down like waters, and righteousness like an everflowing stream."

The biblical concept of justice is also focused on bringing people into right relationship with each other, which Larry Graham calls "relational justice" in *Care of Persons, Care of World*. Justice in relationships is "characterized by shared power, shared opportunity, and shared rewards." Relational justice expresses God's love and justice by "seeking mutuality and reciprocity rather than dominance and subordination" (see chapter 5). Others have called justice between individuals "just love." In summary, love between marriage partners would include a commitment to pursue righteousness and practice justice toward the beloved.

Now we can ask, what are the components of "relational justice" and "just love"? How would this concept inform our relationship to our spouse? We suggest some characteristics of relational justice between marriage partners:

Freedom

God created us with "free will," the freedom and the responsibility to make choices about how we will live our lives. We know only too well that we are determined to some degree by physiological and sociological realities that shape our self. However, within these limitations, and sometimes transcending them, we have the freedom and responsibility to choose. This capacity for self-determination is a gift.

Our faith stresses our responsibility to work at determining God's will for our lives and to live accordingly. Being personally responsible is a major way of maintaining integrity. The more each partner feels in control of her or his own life, the more he or she will be able to give to a relationship characterized by justice and intimacy.

Just love, therefore, recognizes that our spouse, as a child of God, has both the right and the responsibility for self-determination. The loving partner, therefore, will be an advocate for this freedom, the freedom which Paul warned us not to relinquish.

For freedom Christ has set us free. Stand firm, therefore, and do not submit again to a yoke of slavery. (Gal. 5:1)

As our spouse faces decisions about how to exercise this freedom, we will support her or his right to make such choices. We will not attempt to make decisions that rightfully belong to our spouse. We will not try and "run" our partner's life, nor impose our will on her or him.

Empowerment

Beyond support for the expression of our spouse's freedom, just love calls for the intentional empowerment of our partner. Empowerment means working with our partner to enable her or him to develop insight about who he or she is and what he or she is called to be. It means encouragement to claim personal freedom and act on this insight. Just love helps a partner uncover her or his unique gifts and makes space in the relationship for these gifts to be expressed. Enabling the spouse to grow toward psychological and spiritual maturation is one way of advocating freedom.

Kindness

After Micah said that God wants us to "do justice," he added that we were also to "love kindness." In the "love chapter" of 1 Corinthians, Paul says that "love is patient; love is kind; . . ." (1 Cor. 13:4). Linking justice with kindness describes another criteria for assessing just love in your marital relationship. Being kind means foregoing any behaviors that make your spouse feel used or abused. Acts of injustice elicit pain, embarrassment, rejection, and lower self-worth, but just love relates in a manner that promotes a sense of well-being. One way to know that an injustice has occurred is when our partner feels put down, unheard, discounted, or ridiculed. One acceptable way for a husband and wife to be competitive with each other is to see who can express the most kindness!

Faithfulness

Relational justice calls for dealing with the spouse in the context of faithfulness. Identifying with God's righteousness includes a steadfast commitment to covenants. When we promise something to our partner, when we make covenants about the relationship, relational justice demands that we faithfully fulfill them.

Most couples marry with either the implicit or explicit covenant of sexual exclusivity. Affairs are usually destructive because they communicate a lack of integrity in the keeping of the covenant. When mutual agreements, both spoken and unspoken, are broken the angry response is often related to the sense of having been "cheated." That reflects being treated unjustly.

Fairness

When your spouse treats you in a way that you consider unfair, you feel unloved. Deep in our hearts we expect that those who love us will treat us fairly. Just love expresses itself in its concern for equity and fairness.

We know from experience that life is not always fair. However, we do have the power to adopt the doctrine of fairness as a code for marriage and family life. Just love is always moving the relationship toward equality, in which each spouse is sharing the opportunities, privileges, and rewards of marriage as well as the burdens and responsibilities.

Mercy and Forgiveness

The concept of justice is often connected to legalism and punishment for offenders. Just love, however, is always thoroughly integrated with mercy and forgiveness. We understand that our spouses cannot be perfect, nor love us in all the ways we would like to be loved. We accept, therefore, the limitations of being human. We forgive when they are unable to fulfill a commitment or break a covenant, as discussed earlier.

Peace

Justice and peace are closely related. Peace is more likely in relationships and systems in which justice is practiced. The same dynamic is true in marriage. When justice is practiced by both partners, conflict can be minimized and peace can prevail. Why? Justice reduces the number of situations that are "threatening" (see chapter 4) and therefore reduces the amount of anger and conflict which the couple must confront. When principles of justice are in place, managing conflict is much easier.

> BLESSED is the marriage in which both partners
> are committed to justice within the marriage.

If either partner feels hesitant to confront injustice, then its existence will create estrangement and prevent intimacy. A marriage cannot be enriched or move to new levels of intimacy unless perceived injustices are addressed. One covenant that is basic to enrichment of a marriage is the commitment to address perceived injustice between the partners. If you have difficulty communicating and rectifying perceived injustice, seeing a marriage counselor might enable you to understand each other's experience more thoroughly.

PURPOSES BEYOND MARRIAGE

Finding meaning in life is crucial to finding abundant life. Despite major changes in our culture's perception of marriage, we still have cultural myths about the fairy-tale quality of marriage. Many believe that to marry is to find salvation. Somehow the right mate will transport us into the never-never land of bliss and happiness far removed from the realities of daily life. This illusion about marriage not only sets one up for a large dose of disillusionment, but is a theological problem—idolatry. Even a wonderful marriage cannot be the ultimate answer to the foundational spiritual questions about meaning, vocation, faith, salvation, and ethical commitments.

Though marriage is a gift from God and contains wonderful possibilities for love, trust, and ecstasy, marriage is *not* able to construct a larger spiritual meaning for our life. Couples who pursue spiritual growth together will find meaning and happiness in turning their mutual love outward toward others. They will resist the idea that achieving intimacy within a loving relationship is a final end in itself, but recognize that intimacy is an "on the way" goal toward being able to represent God's love and be ministers of reconciliation in the world. Intimate Christian couples have a shared ministry, a commitment to giving themselves to something beyond the relationship. Intimacy forms a solid foundation from which to move into the world on mission.

BLESSED is the couple who have a shared mission.

RENEWAL RITUALS

Covenants in the ancient world of the Hebrews were periodically renewed and celebrated through ceremonies and rituals. Like many couples you probably celebrate your wedding anniversary with a special night out and by exchanging gifts. As relationships evolve the nature of a covenant can change. As a couple advances in psychological and spiritual maturity the nature of their marriage covenant changes.

Some couples have found that rewriting their wedding vows is a meaningful way to acknowledge the sacred dimension of their new commitments. The vows a couple might write for themselves on their tenth or twentieth anniversary can look quite different than those they repeated at their wedding. Others have planned special occasions for celebrating their covenantal commitments.

EXERCISE: Renewed Marriage Vows

As you read, you have been rethinking your ideas about marriage from both psychosocial and theological perspectives. Hopefully you and your spouse have taken time to reshape some of your concepts and change some behaviors as you move toward a more intimate relationship.

1. If you were getting married now, what would you say to one another about your commitments? Take time to capture your new commitments in the form of renewed marriage vows. Take a few days or weeks and write them out.
2. You might take a second step and find a worship context in which to express these vows to one another in the presence of family, friends, the community of believers, and, of course, God.

FOR FURTHER READING

Augsburger, David W. *Helping People Forgive*. Louisville, Ky.: Westminster John Knox Press, 1996.

———. *The Freedom of Forgiveness*. Chicago: Moody Press, 1973.

Moore, Thomas. *Soul Mates*. New York: HarperCollins, 1994.

Smedes, Lewis B. *Forgive and Forget: Healing the Hurts We Don't Deserve*. San Francisco: HarperCollins, 1996.

———. *The Art of Forgiving*. New York: Ballantine Books, 1997.

eight

WHAT DO YOU
AND YOUR PARTNER REALLY NEED?
Making Changes through Covenants

When we choose to marry we are assuming that our partner will be interested in meeting our needs. In fact, it is unlikely that we would choose marriage if courtship did not convince us that this wonderful person could and would meet our needs in the future. Beyond the strong drive to have our own needs met is the "need to be needed," wanting to be important to the person we love and capable of meeting her or his needs. Working to balance our needs with our spouse's needs and respond to both is a major contributor to intimacy.

The word "dependent" has fallen on hard times in our society, becoming a negative word that conveys immaturity and weakness at best, and pathology at worse. But depending on our spouse to meet some of our needs does not make us weak or "needy." To experience love and intimacy to the fullest we must participate in interdependent relationships. We are choosing to depend on this person as part of the need to belong.

The reality is that as humans we have physical, psychological, social, and spiritual needs which can only be met in the context of mutual relationships. The most important of these needs can be called hungers of the heart and spirit. We marry with the expectation that the partnership will "feed" these heart and spirit hungers.

Meeting needs is also important to couples because trust is developed in the process. How does caring lead to trust? If I repeatedly experience care from another person, I begin to believe that my well-being is important to her or him. If I perceive that my well-being is important, then I can trust her or him to relate to me in ways that are supportive, enhancing, and nurturing rather than in ways that would do me harm, or leave me hurting.

Lois continually referred to her difficulty in trusting Brett, yet he had
not done anything that would cause her to think he was unfaithful.
After carefully exploring the situations that led to this sense of mistrust, she was able to identify her concern. Often Brett would agree to
do something for her (pick up something at the store, do a chore
around the house, make a telephone call) as a way of trying to help.
However, he would often forget or not take the time to follow
through. Lois grew up in a divorced family and lived with her mother.
Her separated father often forgot appointments with her or said he
didn't have time. She thought of her father as untrustworthy. She
identified her need to have Brett promise only what he was committed to deliver so that she would not think of him in the same way. As
he changed his behavior, her trust level became stronger and intimacy
developed.

Meeting the other's needs is a tangible way of expressing commitment
and expressing love.

This concept of meeting needs has become a central piece in our marriage enrichment programs because of these obvious connections
between need-meeting, caring, trust, and love. A couple trying to enhance intimacy will choose to identify each other's needs and to adopt
behaviors that meet these needs.

Identifying Needs

Meeting needs is a major way of giving care to our partner, one of
the major characteristics of intimacy. Couples who believe they have
an intimate marriage are committed to mutual need-meeting. They attend to that which enables each partner to find fulfillment and to feel
connected. Loving a spouse, therefore, includes taking seriously her or
his desires and wants. In reality, we often don't find out what our
spouse needs until a conflict occurs and the process of resolution makes
it clear.

Where to start? The preceding chapters have given you an opportunity to identify a number of thoughts and feelings about your marriage.
Many of them are new concepts that provide insight into ways you can
enrich your relationship. Notice that many of your new ideas can be
translated into needs.

First, be clear about your own needs. We are often unaware of our needs, not realizing how they affect our expectations of our spouse.

Juan grew up in a chaotic home with noise and yelling a constant companion. Indecision and uncertainty were always part of the family pattern. When he and his wife, Reba, came for counseling they were in conflict over how to relate to their two young boys. Juan was aware that when there was a lot of noise and confusion he became anxious and frustrated. He was able to identify how strongly he needed peace and stability. Reba listened carefully and committed to working with Juan to find a way to meet these needs. They were able to agree on some changes that would not compromise the normal spontaneity of the children, yet provide a more organized approach to family life.

Second, turn your attention to learning about your partner's needs. Love will motivate you to want to know so you can care in ways that are special to your spouse.

The next exercise may feel risky because you may not have communicated about these needs before. You are making yourself vulnerable to your spouse by identifying your own needs and attempting to identify those of your spouse. We hope you will take the plunge, because working at understanding your needs and your spouse's needs is a caring act.

EXERCISE: Identify the Needs of Both You and Your Partner

In the following exercise you can evaluate your perception of which needs are most important to you and your spouse at this time in life. The exercise will be more helpful if you complete the exercise without discussion. We have listed a number of needs expressed by couples in both therapy and enrichment groups. Blank lines are left on the bottom for you to name specific needs that are important for you and/or your partner.

First, read through the list and identify which needs are most important to *you* at this time. Many needs are important but we are asking that you limit your choices to seven.

Second, read the list again and choose seven needs that you think are most important to *your partner*.

Leave the assessment part on the right side of the page for later.

When you compare notes remember that the goal of this exercise is to share, interpret, and comprehend rather than to argue and defend. Use the awareness wheel concept from chapter 3 to fully express your thoughts. The goal is to reach a "shared meaning." Concentrate on describing and illustrating your needs as expressed in the exercise so that your partner can understand you. Your spouse may learn something he or she has never known about you and can choose, therefore, to love you in a different manner than previously.

Listen and you might be surprised at what you can learn. Your partner may have identified and interpreted a word or phrase to symbolize something important. Work on understanding "where he or she is coming from" so that you can move into the future with hope for being a more caring partner.

Celebrate the many ways in which you are meeting each other's needs and communicating the love you feel toward one another.

Meeting all of a partner's needs, of course, is impossible. The responsibility would be too much of a burden. We can, however, be involved in enabling our spouse to figure out ways to meet his or her own needs and then function supportively.

Some needs change with age and stage in life. At one point in time a person might need support in finishing a college degree, but that is a time-limited need. During child-rearing years both partners might identify support in parenting as a priority need, but later in life this need may become a lower priority. Other needs remain constant given the uniqueness of a person's story. For example, a husband who has difficulty believing he is adequate may have a consistent need for affirmation. A wife who comes from a chaotic background may have an ongoing need for stability.

How Effective Are the Two of You at the Moment?

A measuring stick by which partners evaluate intimacy is the commitment of their partner to meeting needs. If you perceive that your spouse is interested in attending to your needs, you will consider the relationship more intimate than if needs are not being attended to in a satisfactory manner. So it is important to communicate with each other about how well you feel that needs are being met.

What Do You and Your Spouse Need?

Identify seven needs which are currently strongest for you. Make an "X" in the column "My Needs" by those seven without regard for whether or not the need is being fulfilled.

Now concentrate on what your spouse needs from this relationship. Put a check mark or "Y" in the column "Spouse's Needs" by the seven needs you think most important to her/him at this point in time.

Please use the blank lines at the bottom of the page for adding specific needs that are not covered by this list.

Needs	My Needs	Spouse's Needs	Need Is Being Met Not So Well 1	2	3	Very Well 4	5
support in personal growth/self-discovery							
shared playtime/leisure time/fun							
comfort and understanding							
shared religious values							
more privacy/ "space"							
peace and stability							
adventure and excitement							
to be dependent							
to be special to you							
a trusting, honest relationship							
support of my work/vocation							
acceptance for who/what I am							
significant in-depth communication							
emotional security							
physical touch/affection/tenderness							
to be needed by you							
companionship/time with you							
to share homemaking tasks							
financial security							
respect for my gifts and talents							
shared goals/purposes for the future							
intellectual stimulation							
more sexual involvement							
shared parenting							
forgiveness							
emotional intimacy							
freedom to be independent/be myself							
a community of couple friends							
handling conflict more creatively							
spiritual growth as a couple							

Now put an "X" in the column on the far right to indicate how well the needs you chose for yourself are being met. Then put a check mark or "Y" in the column on the far right to indicate how well the needs which you chose as most important to your spouse are being met.

What Do You and Your Spouse Need?

Identify seven needs which are currently strongest for you. Make an "X" in the column "My Needs" by those seven without regard for whether or not the need is being fulfilled.

Now concentrate on what your spouse needs from this relationship. Put a check mark or "Y" in the column "Spouse's Needs" by the seven needs you think most important to her/him at this point in time.

Please use the blank lines at the bottom of the page for adding specific needs that are not covered by this list.

Needs	My Needs	Spouse's Needs	Not So Well 1	2	3	Very Well 4	5
support in personal growth/self-discovery							
shared playtime/leisure time/fun							
comfort and understanding							
shared religious values							
more privacy/ "space"							
peace and stability							
adventure and excitement							
to be dependent							
to be special to you							
a trusting, honest relationship							
support of my work/vocation							
acceptance for who/what I am							
significant in-depth communication							
emotional security							
physical touch/affection/tenderness							
to be needed by you							
companionship/time with you							
to share homemaking tasks							
financial security							
respect for my gifts and talents							
shared goals/purposes for the future							
intellectual stimulation							
more sexual involvement							
shared parenting							
forgiveness							
emotional intimacy							
freedom to be independent/be myself							
a community of couple friends							
handling conflict more creatively							
spiritual growth as a couple							

"Need Is Being Met" spans the last five columns (Not So Well 1 — Very Well 5).

Now put an "X" in the column on the far right to indicate how well the needs you chose for yourself are being met. Then put a check mark or "Y" in the column on the far right to indicate how well the needs which you chose as most important to your spouse are being met.

EXERCISE: How Are You Doing?

In the exercise above you can assess the degree to which you think these seven important needs are being met for both you and your partner. This is a further step toward identifying ways to change the relationship and promote intimacy. To share such perceptions can feel like complaining or criticizing, but we hope you will take the plunge. Follow the instructions for assessment at the bottom of the exercise. Then return to this page.

Now discuss your assessment with each other. Give specific reasons, where possible, for your assessment. Use what you have learned about communication in chapter 3 to learn from each other rather than to argue over the marks. Note the connection between the satisfactory meeting of these needs and the degree of caring and intimacy you feel in the relationship.

The long-range goal of this exercise is toÏ identify ways in which you can love and care for each other more effectively by identifying needs that are important to each other. Since you love your partner, this exercise gives you an opportunity to learn how to love her or him in ways that he or she wants to be loved, rather than guessing or assuming how your partner wants to be loved.

Need meeting must feel mutual. That is, when someone is doing all the giving and not having much opportunity to receive, a sense of inequality begins to form. During a crisis, of course, such as loss of employment, illness, pregnancy, or death of a parent, one spouse may have more needs and have little energy to give to the other.

Unmet Needs and Feeling Unloved

Most of us imagine that if our spouse truly loves us he or she will be interested in meeting our needs. Therefore, if our spouse does not function in a manner that meets our needs, we are less convinced of her or his love—which leads to disappointment and distance rather than intimacy. In therapeutic situations dissatisfaction or conflict is frequently related to the perception that a spouse is either disinterested in meeting needs or is outright blocking the meeting of needs.

Liston and Moneen were in marital therapy because of marital unhappiness. Anger between them seemed constant and they were often "bickering." We asked them to identify a recurring situation in which anger occurred. They described the conflict over whether he put the bath mat back on the side of the tub and pulled the curtain closed after showering. Moneen's most obvious need was for a "clean and straight" bathroom. The deeper need, however, was expressed when she was able to say tearfully, "If he loved me like he says he does he would take the five seconds each day that it takes to do something he knows is important to me!" Her need to feel loved was connected to a behavior from her husband that would have met both the surface need for a straightened bathroom and the deeper need to feel loved.

> BLESSED is the couple who give careful
> attention to each other's needs.

MISUNDERSTANDING
OUR PARTNER'S NEEDS

Because we love our spouse does not guarantee that we understand what he or she needs. Most of us, however, imagine that we know what our partner needs and are often surprised when we think we are meeting a need and discover we are not. Why do we make such assumptions?

Our Family Story

Our conscious and unconscious assumptions are based on how significant adults in our history expressed their needs. It is easy to assume that our partner has the same needs (and wants them met in the same way) as our parents or other significant adults. This is particularly true of adults who are/were the same gender as our spouse.

I (Judy) watched my mom fix large, hot meals each evening when my dad came home from work. His physically demanding job in construction left him hungry and ready to eat. When I married it was my assumption that Andy would also need large, hot meals. But he sits all day at a desk, doesn't eat much, and doesn't like really hot food. Even after playing basketball or tennis he is not very hungry. We had many conflicts around my expectation that he was supposed to eat lots of food, as if I was the expert on how much he needed to eat.

It is important to remember the physical and mental uniqueness of our spouse. Watch out for those assumptions that he or she is the same as "so and so" from your growing up days.

Projection

We can be thrown off track by projecting our needs (and how we want these needs met) onto our partner. Most of us tend to assume that the needs we have are the needs that everyone experiences.

Helen needs to be left alone when ill, wanting only minimal service and little company. She doesn't want to talk or listen, or have anybody in the room fluffing her pillow or asking her repeatedly what she wants to eat or drink. It is natural for her to assume that her husband, Roy, wants the same. When he gets sick, therefore, she leaves him alone, bringing only what is necessary and providing little verbal support or conversation about the circumstances. But Roy needs to be attended to when he is sick. He wants to be fed, soothed, commiserated with, and so forth. He feels that Helen ignores him, leaving him feeling uncared for and even abandoned.

Obviously, it is important for us to invite our spouse to name her or his needs clearly so that we can meet them. After all, usually we want to love our spouse in ways that make her or him feel loved.

EXERCISE: What Do You Need When Sick?
Discuss with your partner how you like to be treated when sick. Name the needs. Then learn what your partner likes and needs when sick.

Because of our differences, we may not understand clearly a need expressed by our spouse. It is tempting to disregard that which we don't understand and assume that our partner simply imagines such a need. This response assumes that we are wise enough to know what our partner needs. This approach denies our partner's uniqueness and discounts her or his ability to recognize and express personal needs.

Gender Assumptions

Gender differences can sabotage intimacy. We carry cultural stereotypes about what males and females need from partners, and may be attempting to meet these needs rather than the actual needs which make our partner unique from the stereotypes. We need to check it out and listen to her or his voice.

We should mention gender specific concerns at this point. Andy, like many males, has grown up with what we call "male self-sufficiency syndrome," which results from being taught that as a male he should not be "needy" (which is for wimps). Furthermore, if he did have needs he should handle them by himself. Males, generally speaking, are not as proficient at naming their needs and asking for them to be met. Females, on the other hand, usually have been taught to identify and respond to the needs of males and may be less proficient at identifying and communicating their own needs. In the earlier exercise on identifying needs, was it easier to name your needs or your partner's?

COVENANTS

Now that needs have been identified, you can choose to change behavior in a way that moves toward intimacy. This is not an easy task, but if you are motivated to love your spouse in ways that are meaningful to her or him, it can be done. A process for changing behavior which we find effective in both enrichment and therapy contexts is "covenant making."

In our society agreements are frequently confirmed in a legal manner through contracts. These binding documents have as their purpose holding people accountable for their agreements. If one fails to fulfill a contract, litigation is the response of choice. Recent literature on marriage emphasizes making contracts between partners. But "contract" seems too impersonal and threatens to place partners against each other.

Covenants, however, are promises which are freely given out of a sense of love and commitment. Covenants are not so much an expectation or demand, but a gift to the other. The concept of "covenant" has a long history within the Judeo-Christian tradition in describing mutual commitments between two parties who have pledged their faithfulness not only to the specific agreements, but to the relationship. Contracts can be made between any two persons, but covenants are made between two persons who are committed to love and care for one another.

When contracts are broken a person can be punished. Often the parties do not have a personal relationship. Covenants, however, reflect trust already established between persons who are in a significant relationship. Contracts are of necessity legalistic and rigid, but covenants are dynamic and fluid. They can be adapted to changing circumstances. Couples find that covenants must be continuously renegotiated to stay current with their life situation. When covenants aren't kept we will probably feel hurt and angry. Unlike contracts, however, when a covenant is broken we can express mercy and forgiveness.

ENTERING A COVENANT

The following process has guided many couples in arriving at covenants. It may feel artificial at first, but after you use this process a few times it becomes easy.

EXERCISE: Making a Covenant

Choose a need which one or both of you marked in the preceding exercise as only "moderately met" and follow these procedures.

1. Make an Appointment

The covenanting process is not one that can be accomplished quickly. Describe to your spouse that you need to share some important thoughts and feelings that you think will enrich the relationship. Invite your partner to work with you on the issue. Set a specific time when the two of you can have an opportunity for uninterrupted conversation.

2. Set the Scene

Agree that the answering machine will be on, the TV off, and plans made for the children (if there are any). Ask for a few minutes to express yourself without interruption or feedback from your partner.

Confirm that you are taking responsibility for identifying your needs and want to invite her or him to join you in discovering a resolution that will contribute to intimacy.

3. Describe Your Perceptions of the Need, Issue, Frustration, or Concern

Using the awareness wheel as explained in chapter 3, carefully describe what you know about your need. Include the information that provides the context for this need, your interpretations of where this need comes from and what it means, the emotion that develops around it, and the actions you would like to consider.

4. Work toward a Shared Meaning

Before working toward a solution make sure you have reached a "shared meaning" as described in chapter 3. Having a shared meaning means asking your spouse to give feedback about what you have shared. Then you can know whether he or she has heard accurately. You may need to repeat, or expand, your description of the need. The goal of this process is to make sure you are both "on the same page" and are addressing the same issue as you move through the process.

5. Brainstorm about Possible Changes of Behavior

After identifying the needs, both of you can bring your creative imagination into play as you consider a variety of possible actions which could meet this need. Don't settle on the first idea; the obvious one might not be the most creative. As the partner expressing the need you may have fantasized a particular change which you imagine will fix everything, but your partner needs to participate in making suggestions. Make sure to image a variety of scenarios which might work.

6. Agree on a Plan of Action

Choose one from all the possibilities and turn it into a carefully crafted plan of action. Remember that this plan of action must be one that both partners can agree to keep. If the plan is not mutual, then the plan is doomed to fail because of one partner's resentment. One of you may be agreeing to an action plan that calls for a change of behavior that you would rather not change. Out of love for your partner, however, you are willing to change for the length of the covenant to see if this change will bring about a desired result.

Attend to the details and anticipate as many problems as possible, so that the covenant has every chance to work.

> When Arlene and Jonathan agreed to meet their joint need to spend more time as a couple, they made a covenant to spend Friday nights together. They attended to many details, deciding who would arrange for a baby-sitter, how they would take turns planning the evening (so they wouldn't get stuck in the "Where do you want to go?"/"It doesn't matter to me" debate), and what time they would commit to being ready to leave.

The plan of action must include specific action, rather than generalized ideas, so that both partners can be clear about whether or not the covenant has been kept. Evaluation will be impossible if specific behaviors cannot be measured (see below). A plan of action, therefore, cannot contain the word "try" because it is difficult to measure how much a partner "tried." How can you measure "we will try and spend more time together"? But if the decision is to have time together on Friday evenings for the next three weeks from 7:00 to 10:00, then you will know after three weeks whether you kept the covenant or not.

7. Write Down the Plan/Covenant

As strange as it may seem, couples can have conflict over their covenant, particularly if one spouse has agreed to make a significant behavior change. Forgetting or misunderstanding the specific terms of the covenant can occur. Therefore, writing down the details of the plan of action serves several functions.

First, seeing the covenant on paper gives it a sense of particularity that spoken words lack, driving home the reality of the commitment. Second, if the couple is uncertain about the specific decisions, or even in disagreement about them, the written form serves as a reference. We (Judy and Andy) keep our covenants on a three-by-five card in the top drawer of the dresser where we can consult the "written document," as we humorously call it.

8. Plan a Time for Evaluation of the Covenant

Covenants must have a set ending time. They cannot be entered for eternity. When we hear a partner, or a couple, say something like, "From now on I/we will . . ." we intervene. "From now on" is a long time and finite limitations make it difficult to know how well we will manage a change in behavior. Covenants are best made for a limited amount of time, probably a few weeks.

At the end of the specified time a careful evaluation must be made. Did we follow the action plan? Was our purpose accomplished? Did we run into unexpected problems? Then, on the basis of a careful assessment, the covenant can be continued as is, renegotiated to correct unforeseen problems or newly recognized possibilities, or dropped in favor of a whole different covenant that would better serve the overall goals.

9. Anticipate Sabotage and Adopt Preventive Measures

After agreeing on a plan of action, writing it down, and planning a time of evaluation, you will find it helpful to explore the idea of sabotage. Frequently the couple will know from past history how each of them is most likely to sabotage the covenant. If the behaviors which could sabotage the covenant are identified in advance and raised to conscious awareness, then preventive steps can be taken.

> We (Judy and Andy) frequently make covenants around setting aside time to talk during the week and keep up-to-date with each other. This time allows us to connect, make decisions, and enjoy each other's companionship. When we raise the sabotage question, I (Judy) am likely to sabotage by continuing to work past the time we have covenanted to meet on the couch for conversation. Simply raising the question keeps me more aware of the time and the commitment.

10. Awareness of God's Presence

Like the vows at our wedding, we can make covenants in God's presence. In a sense we make covenants with the Spirit of God as a confirming and motivating participant. We are saying to our partner, "Because of my commitment to you and to God, I commit to the following." Many couples prayerfully invite God's presence when they begin the covenant-making process. One couple always holds hands after completing the process and asks God's blessing on their covenant.

> BLESSED is the person whose partner is willing to
> make changes in behavior to deepen intimacy.

Note: If you attempt several covenants that are mutual, and continuously fail to keep these covenants, then something is amiss. Commit to discovering and resolving the deeper issues leading to the sabotage (see chapter 4 on anger). If you do not feel in control of your own behavior, give yourself the gift of discussing this with a professional counselor. Seeking a third party to help the process becomes the responsible next step.

FOR FURTHER READING

Hendricks, Gay and Kathlyn. *Conscious Loving: The Journey to Co-Commitment*. New York: Bantam Books, 1990.

Hendrix, Harville. *Getting the Love You Want: A Guide for Couples*. New York: Harper and Row, 1988.

Epilogue

In a perfect situation we would be able to sit with you and have leisurely conversation about your experiences with the ideas we discuss in this book. We would enjoy hearing your responses to the exercises and exploring your questions. We would enjoy watching your facial expressions as you make a new discovery about each other. It would be an honor to walk with you through the process of finding new life within your relationship. Most of all we would delight in sharing your pleasure at the new and deeper experiences of love and intimacy.

We are grateful that you choose to be intentional in exploring the rich possibilities that God has made possible within a committed marriage. We know that God's grace will embrace the two of you as you continue your pilgrimage into intimacy.